Performing Arts in the Primary School

Performing Arts in the Primary School

PAULINE TAMBLING

BLACKWELL EDUCATION

© Pauline Tambling, 1990
First published 1990

Published by
Basil Blackwell Ltd
108 Cowley Road
Oxford OX4 1JF
UK

British Library Cataloguing in Publication Data
Tambling, Pauline
    Performing arts in primary school. – (Primary matters)
    1. Primary Schools. Activities. Performing arts
    I. Title II. Series
    372.6'6

    ISBN 0-631-17364-1
    ISBN 0-631-16423-5 (Pbk)

Typeset in Century Schoolbook 11/13 pt by Times Graphics, Singapore.
Printed in Great Britain by Dotesios (Printers) Ltd, Trowbridge.

Contents

Acknowledgements

All the projects and ideas in this book are descriptions of work in schools that I have been associated with through my work for the Royal Opera House. I am particularly grateful to JoAnn Forman and Bruce Taylor from the Metropolitan Opera Guild, in New York. JoAnn and Bruce originated a way of working with young children for opera and ran courses at the Royal Opera House. Many of the projects described here resulted from their courses. They introduced me to the idea of using the professional model of theatre organisation with children, a model used by many British theatre education programmes now.

I would particularly mention some teachers with whom I have enjoyed working and whose projects are described:

Carol Smith and Felsted Primary School in Essex

Pat Curtis, Jo Simpson and Lesley Funge, Bishops' Tachbrook School in Leamington Spa

Val Brodie, Gwen Proudlock, David Drake, Deirdre Rider, Robina Nicolson, Avril Lethridge and Badgemore Primary School in Henley.

The musical ideas were involved by Edward Lambert during various projects for the Royal Opera. Richard Gregson's work on stage direction and Paa 'C' Quaye as a professional writer have helped me formulate ideas in these areas.

The illustrations on stage design are by Robin Auld.

I would also mention Maurice Anderson with whom I first organised performance projects at Kirby-le-Soken Primary School in Essex, Henry Pluckrose who initiated this book and has given encouragement and valuable advice throughout its preparation, Leone Burton whose comments were always useful and, most of all, I would like to thank my husband Jeremy.

Primary Matters: Editors' Preface

It is hard to find an acknowledgment of how recent are primary schools whose curriculum and management reflects the particular emotional, social, intellectual and physical needs of young children nor of how far they have developed in a very brief time span. Indeed, there are teachers in today's primary schools who remember that in 1949, five years after the famous Butler Education Act, 36% of children of secondary age were still attending schools which also housed children under 11. Those same teachers have seen the development of primary schools through the Plowden era in the 1960s, the building of open-plan schools which aroused such intense international interest in the 1960s and '70s, into the 1980s and the new Act introducing a national curriculum and attainment targets for children of 7 and 11 years.

In the years following the First World War, successive government committees examined the educational needs of adolescents, of boys and girls in the middle years of childhood (7–11) and of children of 'infant and nursery' age. These committees reported between 1926 and 1933; their recommendations, though implemented in a piece-meal fashion, led to a considerable restructuring of schooling in England and Wales. The most profound effect of these changes was the acknowledgement that the primary years were a coherent and essential stage in the educational process, a stage which had distinctive needs and requirements. Prior to this, children had been educated in all-age schools. Unless a child were fortunate enough to be selected at the age of 11 (usually as a successful outcome of academic competition), the school she joined at 5 years of age would be the school s/he left at 13. Ninety per cent of the school population attended such schools and it became increasingly obvious that they were failing simultaneously to meet the differing needs of the 5-year-old, the child in the middle years, and of the 13-year-old school leaver. In the late 1930s, primary schools began to develop, with secondary(elementary) schools providing for those children who failed the selective examination. The distinctive categories of secondary education were enshrined in the 1944 Education Act which established a comprehensive tri-partite system of secondary education, but even five years later this was still not fully realised.

It took, therefore, some twenty years from the mid-1930s for primary schools to become generally established and, with the population explosion of the 1950s and '60s, primary school practice underwent many developments as the early years of schooling came to be regarded as an essential phase in the educational process. Experiments were undertaken in teaching and learning methodology in the curriculum, in the organisation of classes (remember vertical or family grouping?), and, as already mentioned, in the architectural style of new schools. The curriculum became richer and more challenging to young children. Enthusiastic support for these changes was found in the report published by the Plowden Committee in 1967.

In contrast to this period, more recently primary education has been subject to critical appraisal and retrenchment. Academics (like Peters and Dearden) and politicians (like Boyson and Cox), as well as Inspectors from local education authorities and Her Majesty's Inspectorate, have focused attention upon the issues and assumptions underlying the work offered by teachers to young children. Are there things which *all* children should learn during their primary years? What constitutes essential knowledge for the primary-aged child? What should be the balance between the teaching of facts, the development of skills, the understanding of the concepts which underlie knowledge, and the processes through which this knowledge is acquired and developed? How effective are different classroom approaches in developing thinking skills, social awareness and responsibility? How can the primary curriculum best address the fundamental technological changes brought about by the microchip? In what ways are social issues such as racism, sexism or disadvantage best addressed? How should the particular insights and experiences of the disabled child be incorporated? How can institutional barriers to the involvement of all interested parties, especially parents, in the education of each child be dismantled? How should religious education be handled within a society which is more and more secular but also no longer made up of only one major faith group?

Questions such as these are not asked in a vacuum. They reflect the anxieties (real and imagined) of parents, academics, politicians, industrialists and, most of all, of the teachers themselves. That such questions are now being asked is, in part, a recognition of how far primary schools have come over the fifty or so years since they were first conceived. In a climate of concern and criticism, it is also easy to forget that British developments in primary education have been the focus of attention, respect and emulation in many other countries. Indeed, many have argued that it was a freedom from bureaucracy which gave English primary schools their unique character and made possible the kinds of thoughtful experiment which attracted an international reputation. At the same time, others have suggested that piecemeal development has led to idiosyncracy. Hence the current demand for every school to follow a programme reflecting clearly defined national criteria. However, the need for the individual teacher to make choices, ask questions, and influence every child's development continues to be respected and, however centralised the curriculum may become, however much the school programme is evaluated, however regularly children are tested against performance norms, the thoughtful teacher will continue to ask questions about *what* John or Akbar, Mary or Mai-Lin will learn, how they will learn it, what particular needs they have and how their individual interests, attitudes and aptitudes can be accommodated into the daily work of the classroom.

All the books in this series address aspects of these kinds of questions which teachers are asking as part of their concern to establish effective strategies for learning. Part of that concern focuses upon the links between the excitement of learning evidenced by young children, and the need to evaluate and maintain coherence in their experiences. Effective learning is the product of engagement as each and every member of the group struggles to make the learning process her or his own. At the same time, personal learning can still be limited unless it is placed in a broader context so that, for example, subject strands unite into a comprehensible and rational whole. Each author in this series seeks to indicate cross-curricular links, even though the titles indicate particular subject specialisms as starting points, so that the approach unifies rather than divides the child's experience of the curriculum.

As editors of this series, we wish to present to practising primary teachers a range of titles which recognises the complexity of the primary teacher's role. Each book will give shape and purpose to specific curriculum areas, dealing with issues which are particular to that specialism, presenting ideas for interesting and innovative practice in that area but, at the same time, emphasising the unity of the primary experience. Thus each title is set against a broad canvas, that of the primary school as a living and vibrant place in which young children grow and learn.

Leone Burton
Henry Pluckrose

1 What are the performing arts?

People of all backgrounds and cultures share an enthusiasm for and history of performing. The many stories of the past have, over the centuries, been relayed to new generations through drama, art, music and dance. Often stories have been approached through different art-forms, and indeed, re-worked or adapted for new generations. An example of a well-known story in the European tradition would be Cinderella. The piece is typical pantomime material telling the story, originally by Charles Perrault, of Cinderella (from *Contes de ma mére l'oye* 1697), the badly treated step-sister of the two ugly sisters, who, in many pantomime re-workings goes to the ball, falls in love with Prince Charming and is later traced by the fitting of a lost shoe by the prince who then marries her. The 'bones' of the story have been adapted time and time again in the theatre and in books and form part of the range of stories of which most European children are aware. In addition several choreographers have used the bones of the story to create ballets, with the Prokofiev score probably the most famous, and certainly in Britain the choreography of Sir Frederick Ashton for the Royal Ballet the most well known. There have been several operatic treatments of variations on the story too, most famously Rossini's *Centerentola* (1817). And, of course, there are regular re-interpretations for Christmas pantomime presentations both professional and amateur. Non-European cultures boast an equally rich fund of stories that have been retold and written over many years.

Each generation has created its own theatre which is of particular relevance to its time and people, and which has celebrated, challenged or explored aspects of human relationships, ideas and society. Many examples of such works are lost to us but societies have selected some to preserve and we can, in a small way, glimpse the theatre of the past. The Cinderella story itself, though simple, raises all sorts of questions about personal morality and family life, and the fact that it has been reworked so often suggests that there is something of long-term interest in the tale.

In schools children are exposed to an educational process which attempts to teach skills and facts but has the primary task of preparing children to live in today's society. Such 'living' is not merely 'working', and education is not just training but should reflect a variety of human activities: practical skills to be used in adult working life and leisure activities such as sports and arts. The arts, both performing arts and individual artforms, such as painting or music, offer technical skills and an opportunity to look at the concerns and interests of writers, composers and visual artists. Schools can provide a focus for children to perform and to enquire into the works of contemporary artists and those from the past. 'Performing' is a very important aspect of adult life. Children are aware of performers on TV, street players and pop culture. Some, through their parents, experience theatre, cinema and 'live' performances.

This book will deal with performance arts in primary schools. It will also try to bridge the gap between the end-of-term production, which for many conscientious teachers is an annual headache, and the creative arts in the classroom; often the two are unrelated but with a small amount of organisation it is possible that an educationally sound programme of classroom work can enhance and even become such a 'production'. There are many aspects of professional theatre practice that relate directly to primary school work and so by combining the professionalism of theatre organisation with the need to extend performing arts work in schools beyond just acting and singing, there is scope for a new and imaginative combination of the two.

The 'performing arts' is a broad area which includes obviously linked and unlinked subject areas. It also cuts across other subject barriers in that it both enhances learning in some areas and depends on skills taught in others. National Curriculum guidelines tend to be grouped by 'subject' and teachers might feel inclined to organise their class teaching by subject rather than along broader curriculum lines. In the HMI series *Curriculum matters: The curriculum from 5 to 16* (1985) certain broad headings for skills learning are introduced. These include 'communication skills', 'problem-solving skills', 'creative and imaginative skills' all of which are well served by an integrated pattern of learning that cuts across subject boundaries. Primary school teachers are highly skilled at relating goals achieved to meet the assessment requirements of each subject area for the National Curriculum. By using the arts to make such skill acquisition relevant, the results of the arts projects will ensure achievement way above the minimum requirements. The same publication also suggests that 'Skills are best acquired in the course of activities that are seen as worthwhile in themselves'. Arts projects always are and bring with them a context for learning.

As an example of the arts servicing other areas, take a theme like 'Characters' and explore how it can be dealt with through the performing arts.

1   Invent characters by creating characteristics. Character A is witty, confident, caring, honest and tactless. Even this very basic beginning can lead to a good deal of language work. Can the character be both caring and tactless? Why is the character so confident? What does this character need in his or her friends? How does Character A relate to Character B who is friendly, shy, clever, indecisive and stubborn?
2   Thinking about relationships between characters in this way can lead quite naturally to role play. Imagine that you are Character A and you have just met Character B in the playground. Character B is new to the school today... Already the children involved in the role-play can begin to identify with the characters and see life from their viewpoint.
3   How do the characters dress? Here there's an opportunity for elementary costume design and textiles work. Why would Character B wear a particular garment? Where would Character A shop?
4   Where do the characters live? Which shapes or colours could represent them? What are their bedrooms like? This leads into art and mathematics.
5   What sounds could represent them? What sort of music could be composed to illustrate their characters? Here's a place for music.
6   What types of movement might represent them? (dance and PE).

By asking a series of simple questions we have already cut across several subject barriers. Language work is enhanced along with writing as well as the more obvious subject areas. Also, because the theme deals with characters with ordinary characteristics, the children can identify with them. They are relevant to their own experience with people.

We could progress a stage further by making models of the characters' rooms and move into craft and mathematics through scale drawing, 3D presentations and set design. An improvised scene like this can be presented to another group of children as a performance. To present a scene on stage it can be helpful to use simple stage lighting. Even three stage lights of the type normally found in schools present simple scientific problems: should coloured gels be used? Can different atmospheres be created using different colours? If three lights are used, how does the scene look with one light behind the actors and two in front of them? What about three lights from the front? Different combinations can be tried practically and the results recorded.

Obviously with such diversity this work cannot be left only to the specialist music teacher. Every classroom teacher can develop an approach to the performing arts and can use them both as a method of presenting work to others (e.g. in the school assembly) or as a particular performing arts project. It is sad that many primary school teachers feel unqualified to deal with arts subjects. Research[1] shows that the arts are under-represented in pre-service teacher training and there is often a shortage of music and other arts specialists in primary schools, but that classroom teachers are often excellent teachers of the performing arts, as this is, in many ways, an extension of normal curriculum planning and can be a liberating body of work for even the relatively inexperienced classroom teacher. There is a severe shortage of specialists in music, art, dance and drama in our schools. However, it is evident that any performing arts programme should reach as many children as possible and should not be restricted to the availability of a specialist teacher once or twice each week. This is not to underestimate the valuable work of specialists. A balance of specialist work and arts work across the curriculum is called for, with enthusiastic teachers taking responsibility for their own pupils' arts experiences and, to some extent, for their own professional development in the area of arts teaching.

The 'performing arts' grow from the 'contemplative' arts such as writing and painting which can also be shared through performance or exhibition. Writing prose or poetry and painting are accepted as a valid part of the primary school curriculum. Many would say that education for such arts seeks out the 'humanness' of the child: to look inside and to draw out innate creativity. Often the performing arts do this, but they also offer a tool for dealing with issues, emotions and ideas that have to do with the individual coming to terms with others (peers, family, society). They provide a vehicle for sharing something that is common to a group rather than exhibiting the 'me-ness' of the child. When developing a new script or score, children will often find that there are issues in which they share an interest: playground bullying, conflict, attitudes of adults to children, unfairness. Such concerns provide a focus for discussion, expression and communication.

For example, in a class of 7 to 8 year olds, the children wrote a script about the attitudes of parents to children. The children were concerned that parents cared about their material welfare (buying them clothes and food) but didn't register their emotional needs. Central to the plot was a moment when some of the characters knew from the parents of the central character that they had planned a secret swimming pool outing as a surprise birthday present for their daughter. All the children knew that the girl was afraid of water and hated swimming lessons at school. The parents in planning the surprise had completely failed to realise their daughter's feelings. This material provoked an enormous amount of classroom discussion. The children were able to dicuss the issue from their own viewpoints and the teacher was able to broaden the discussion and to point out the parents' position. In arriving at the situation itself the group discussed different situations that might have arisen in the family before deciding on the swimming pool option. There was a good deal of comment on why the parents behaved as they did, why the daughter had not told the parents of her fears, whether the other children should tell their friend what was planned or the parents the problem. Throughout the discussion process there were opportunities for role play when a group of six or seven children could imagine themselves in the same situations and consider how they would react. This early writing aspect of the performing arts is often neglected in favour of putting on an existing play or musical.

Performing arts cover the broad areas of dance, music and drama (and could include film and video which are not dealt with here). Indeed any form that allows expression or communication would come under this heading. Such communication is not necessarily verbal but can be through sound, visuals, shape or movement.

In looking at the curriculum we can identify four aspects. The performing arts are essentially made up of:

- creative work
- recreation (or interpretation)
- craft and skills
- critical skills.

Creative work

'Creative' has been a buzz word in curriculum development circles for a long time and while many teachers agree that it is an important element of education, very little of practical value is available in book form. Creative work often relies on the skill of the teacher in responding to the ideas of the children, rather than a pupil text book or worksheet. Often 'creative' work in class can seem pointless to the pupils who perceive it as an exercise that is quite unrelated to what they expect of music, dance or art. Pupils' experience of the peforming arts will often come from seeing professional performers on television or, occasionally, through live theatre, and it is important for them to see the link between classroom music, dance or drama and the 'real thing'. This is why it is helpful to work towards a 'showing of work' even if no performance is envisaged. 'Product' is important to children and indeed, anyone in adult life. At the other extreme there is the school play which obviously relates to what the pupils understand to be 'drama', but to perform a West End musical is of dubious educational value. Certainly the children involved will acquire certain skills such as learning to work together and production technique but will they as individuals gain more than confidence? Important though this is, it is insufficient to justify the time and effort involved as often the only result is the performance.

Professionally in arts education there is a strong commitment to learning through drama where children explore topics and ideas through improvisation and this will be discussed in a later chapter. Unfortunately there is an assumption that the practices of profes-sional theatre organisation have no place in the classroom. There are, however, ways of uniting the educational aims of 'learning through experience' with professional theatre practice, to provide another way of working. Throughout this book three areas will be kept in mind:

- theatre and the arts as the property of the class or child (how can the child use them for his or her own expression?)
- learning *through* drama, dance or music
- enjoying the work of others in performance and using dance, music and drama as a starting point for classroom work.

When we look at our aims in the performing arts in schools, a primary objective is to provide a vehicle for **expression** and **communication**. By using these terms it is not assumed that every performance has a blatant message, but rather that it is possible for children to use dance, drama or theatre as a medium for expression. It is important, too, that such expression is not necessarily reading or narrative based: reading and writing are often later develop-ments. Young children happily use painting and drawing early on in their school lives. They can also be encouraged to dance and make music as valid forms of expression in their own right and not only as illustrations of narrative writing. Similarly, if use of visual representation, expression through drama and music and dance are given status throughout the child's schooling there will be a seriousness about arts work at all levels. There is a hidden curriculum in the way we treat these skills. Are drawing and painting seen as valuable only in the infant department or until the child is a fluent writer? Are picture books given only to small children? A visual artist can communicate to young children, older children and adults. The skills to be learnt in music, drama and dance are not pleasures to be grown out of. Chapter 2 *The child as communicator and creator* will examine the nature of creative work in more detail.

Re-creative work

A second element is interpretation: a skill that comes with experience of life and is, therefore, hardest to use with infants. However all primary children can gain a great deal from discussion around the subject of acting. One class of infants dealing with their own material were extremely competent when asked to imagine themselves as particular characters. This enabled them to understand the feelings of other characters in the piece that they had written. The teacher would say 'Imagine that you are LeRoy' and the children would be able to put themselves in his position and answer quesions about why he had done certain things. Questioning went along the lines of 'How did he feel when the other children wouldn't play with him?' or 'Why did he befriend Darren?': The children could 'become' LeRoy in turn and could discuss his situation in an informed way. Preliminary discussion and role-play with the group over several sessions ensured that the characters who eventually appeared on the stage were well developed and 'rounded' characters. Also spreading the work over a few days enabled the children to think about the characters between sessions.

Original creative work of this sort can have a longer life than performance by its creators and can be passed on to others to perform. Often young children can delight in seeing and hearing their own compositions or character interpreted by other, perhaps older, children with more technical skill. Older children can enjoy seeing professionals interpret their work. Recreative work (or performance) enables discussion on intent and meaning. In the example above the painstaking background work in evolving the character of LeRoy resulted in just a few lines that the actor actually said on stage. The 'creators' knew the character of LeRoy well enough to improvise on stage. Although they kept to the script they were able to respond to the character by knowing the background research that had gone into the rehearsals. Later the teachers wrote down the script and gave it to a second group who performed it. When another child tackled the role of LeRoy later, his first job was to study the lines to try to work out some of the background that the writers had put into the character. The interpretation was, of course, quite different. Older children will appreciate the role of the interpreter (actor, musician, dancer) more clearly if they are used to seeing their own creative work performed in this way. They will soon see the need to learn a method of communicating their ideas through notation (not necessarily conventional notation), stage directions, video etc. The need for such recording can justify learning these skills.

It is essential to distinguish interpretation from the creative process so that each child becomes aware of the necessity to communicate how something should be performed. It is also interesting for children to learn, quite early on, that any creative work can be changed, edited or enhanced by different interpreters. Here is an example of a very straightforward scene written by a group of 12 to 13 year olds.

Granny's dead

KATE   Thank goodness you're here. I thought Mum and Dad were going to rush off and leave me on my own — you took ages coming home.

JOHN   Well, they didn't believe me at first — and how they argued.

KATE   Well, that's nothing new.

CLAIRE   How did Grandma die?

KATE   I think she had a heart attack, the hospital said she died in the ambulance on the way.

FAITH   I hope Grandpa isn't too upset. Where are they going to take him?

KATE   I don't know. Maybe they'll take him to Auntie Doreen's — 'cos it's so nice and quiet there.

FAITH   Do you think we ought to go to this disco tonight? After all Grandma has just died.

KATE   Well, Mum and Dad said that it would take your minds off it all. Grandma wouldn't have wanted you to be miserable and miss a party.

CLAIRE   We'll decide later on.

KATE   Don't forget Mum and Dad said we've all got jobs to do. John — you've got to clean out your hamster —

you haven't done it for ages.

FAITH   Yes, it's about time you did it — it's beginning to smell.

JOHN   Well, I can't. I've just washed my hands ready to play on the computer — last time someone had got it sticky and I've cleaned it all up.

CLAIRE   I've never known a boy so clean — you're always either in the bath or on the computer.

JOHN   Well at least I'm not dirty.

FAITH   Well your hamster certainly is so go and do it.

The writers of the scene had a particular interpretation in mind and when the play was originally performed they played it in the way the writers had conceived it. At a later stage in a teacher workshop (with stage director, Bruce Taylor, working with the Metropolitan Opera Guild), a group of 12 teachers worked on the scene in three groups. None of the teachers knew anything about the original play, nor the intention of the writers in putting the script together. The director asked the groups to prepare the scene in three very different ways: the first as if the characters were children of about the age of the writers, the second as if the characters were related adults and the third as if they were unrelated adults. The three scenes were 'blocked' in exactly the same way but the result was completely different. The third group had to deal with the problems particular to its brief: 'Granny' became the pet name of a landlady with whom they once had rooms. The children would have been surprised to see how much could be made of such a simple scene, but all writing (including music and choreography) works in this way and requires interpretation. The interpreters bring their own skill to the writing, composition and dance. In an age where so many sound and video works exist, it is a pity that there is not more understanding about the differences in interpretation between players, dancers and conductors. Even adults tend to think of a particular recording of a piece of music as representing the work itself.

With older children, work on interpretation can lead to a natural need for tape or video recordings of their work so that it can be preserved in some form. Just as the status of painting is enhanced by mounting and display so it is useful to allow a created piece of music or dance some length of life beyond the performance. Children can be allowed to record a certain number of pieces throughout the school year. These can be reviewed at the end of the year so that there is an overview of achievement. Imagine how satisfying it is to see that work done in an earlier class still has value: when children write books for younger children to read or when a song is sung by others, it is very exciting for the creator and denotes 'real' value. Also the creator can see opportunities for developing ideas in subsequent work by understanding how others deal with it.

Craft and skills

The technical and skills aspect of arts work is the most concrete. In any group of young people some will be attracted to the practical 'making' side and all will benefit from skill development. Arts work is developmental and only by marrying creative work and technical expertise can real progress be made. Musical 'improvisation' has sometimes attracted disapproval because it is perceived as totally spontaneous whereas, properly employed, each improvisation task builds on the one before so that highly skilled performers are encouraged to take part in improvisation sessions and not just newcomers. Skills training for performing music, drama and dance is important. Additionally there are practical aspects of stagecraft that can be learnt. Children enjoy making props, scenery and working on costume or lighting design. Mask-making, carpentry, puppet-making can all be built into an arts curriculum. Another practical skill is the running of a performance: management on stage, organisation of a production, and the various aspects of telling others about it, advertising, making programmes etc. This is very popular with children because it has an aim (to complete a task) and an obvious end (the object or job done). There is also a sense of achievement and value to the end result. It is better still to incorporate the activity into a longer project involving both creative and interpretive activities. This area is most interesting because it allows the possibility of developing areas of craft work along professional lines so that the processes of set design or prop making can reflect those developed in the professional theatre. This will be discussed in more detail later. If possible it is very exciting to let the craft aspect of a project 'feed into' the creative ideas of a project, so that the practical aspect does not merely service the creative side. Poster designs can influence set design which in turn can affect drama improvisation.

Critical skills

If one is thorough with the processes above, this section will look after itself. If children are fully involved in these proceses they will not need extensive notes to read before going to the theatre or an elaborate talk before seeing the work of others. In fact 'learning about' can easily be replaced by 'learning through experience'. Children will understand author intention and will be able to evaluate the skills of the performers and technical crew if they have taken on those roles themselves. They will not talk in vague terms about a performance being 'pretty' or 'boring' but, through doing, will have gained the valuable key to understanding the work of others. In fact it is crucial to note that going to a performance of any artistic piece (or another class piece) is not about mere enjoyment ('letting the piece wash over') but is about genuine and critical watching. If children can learn to ask intelligent and practical questions about a production, they are moving towards a real understanding of what is involved in theatre, while simultaneously developing their critical thinking. Such questions might query particular lighting effects or motivation of character and are rarely bland statements.

The necessity to provide 'role-models' (or examples of good practice) of theatre cannot be over-emphasised. Too often children identify performing arts as being on a similar scale to learning nursery rhymes, that is, something learned when very young or in primary school and therefore something to grow out of. It is essential to extend the range of experiences by exposing children who compose, play or dance to the work of other children and to professional artists. Such contact provides motivation for future work. In this context, the commitment to continue an arts programme throughout the primary and seconday school will ensure that the arts will not be perceived as 'just another project' like 'transport' or 'the sea' but as a valid part of life and living . Also a constant need to improve, gain new skills, try different ideas and techniques will be generated.

A visit to see a professional production requires funding and inconvenience in terms of rescheduling the school day and is, therefore, a very special occasion. When it forms part of a longer performing arts project it is far more valuable that just an outing. If it is not possible to go to see a live production with the children, there are plenty of video productions available now, and, of course, productions on television which can be enjoyed as a group.

Some ground rules

In designing a performing arts programme for a school, some important points need consideration. When a professional theatre company mounts a production, the motivating force behind all those involved in the show is the first night. Without it the people involved would neither be able to do their jobs properly nor work effectively as a team. The deadline is the one thing that keeps a coherence between the actors, management, craftspeople and the promotion machinery. Without it the publicity would fall apart, the audience remain unaware of the performances and the actors have no incentive to rehearse. In all education children should respond to *real tasks* in order to ensure *real achievement*.

The performing arts have real deadlines – performances or perhaps a 'showing' or 'sharing of work'. There is a subtle balance to be achieved between process and product. From the teacher's viewpoint the process can be successful without the performance or 'end result' but this is not true for the children. Too often children are involved in either *process* (a project) or *product* (often the 'school production'). With National Curriculum criteria in mind teachers have less and less time for extra curricular activities such as the school production. With the performing arts working across the curriculum, presentations and performances can evolve naturally from classroom work. Without the performance there is no reality for the children and without the learning process there is no point in a project for the teacher. Artificial creativity is meaningless and an end of term 'revival' is pointless educationally. For example, when asked what was important about their production of a musical piece about classroom bullying, a group of top juniors said 'It was the first time we finished something'. In fact this wasn't the case, as many projects in which the class had been involved, had been completed in the teacher's terms. Unfortunately the children had not perceived them in the same way. For them the performance and the resulting status of their work was all-important and would affect future work and their attitudes to it. On the other hand an end-of-term production can be tremendously exciting for the students without impinging on classroom work at all.

All performing arts should be *progressive*, building on what has been done before, not, as often happens, in dance particularly, that children of 8 and 11 years are basically working in exactly the same way technically but with new stories. Experience and skill learning are vital to the maturing of arts output. Every task should be more demanding than the one before. Each term of study should bring with it new skills, different and challenging media, better technique which can serve the pupil. Similarly, music teachers can point to new instruments, different compositional techniques and new listening, to widen horizons as much as possible throughout a planned programme. Take an example of a dance project. A group of children worked over several weeks on the creation of a score and of choreography on the subject of the seasons: summer, autumn, winter and spring. Colours and appropriate movements and shapes (spiky, icy shapes for winter, for example) were ascribed to each and the children worked out music and movement to represent the seasons over four five-minute pieces. When tackling a second project the temptation might be to repeat the formula but, perhaps, take a new theme (the elements would be an example). In doing this, the subject matter of the new project would be different, but the outcome would probably be very similar and there would be a danger of it not being as good as the original project. It would be important to add a new dimension in a second project: to takle the problems of narrative dance or to work on the ideas evolved in the first project. Throughout there needs to be a balance between technical development and overall project aims. The pressure to overcome difficulties should be met 'head on' when required but should service the child's educational needs.

Frameworks can be fixed so that within a given structure the child can have total freedom and can be sure that the structure is safe and will work. It is particularly important for less able children to succeed, as confidence is extremely valuable for future success. In the above example a second project could be set in one of the four seasons of the first project, so that the movements can be developed and extended. Here are just two ideas for possible development.

- a new dimension. A shadow could be introduced to explore the idea of working in pairs as a mirror. The shadow could disappear in winter or the winter scene could be set indoors.
- the four presentations could be linked by an individual who moves from scene to scene.

The teacher will gradually gain confidence in trying out new ideas which extend the children's technical skills.

1   The starting point for any work in this area has to be grounded in *what the children already know.* Children bring their own knowledge and past experience which can be from any cultural or social background. Often the starting point is what the teacher feels will be accessible: easy classical styles in music, rondo form etc. Most young people listen to many hours of music each week and their tastes can be complex. It is more important to start with a known musical style and develop from there rather than find a simple but irrelevant starting point. Structures can be simple but content need not necessarily be so. The problems of dealing with European musical styles in multi-

cultural contexts can easily be avoided by allowing children to start from their own experience: many urban classrooms can boast a wealth of cultural experience which is a rich starting point for the performing arts. Stories and music from home can enhance classroom work. There need be no fear of tackling subject matter unfamiliar to the teacher. It is the *skills* and *structure* that the teacher offers and the richer the source material the better. The Opies' books *Children's games in street and playground* and *Language and the lore of schoolchildren*[2] are worth reading, as are the many collections of stories from all cultural backgrounds.

2 In all projects a sense of *sharing with others* either in performance or by sharing between groups within a class is important. Any competition in the arts is alien to good practice. Although individuals can compete outside the classroom in terms of technical ability, a creative arts piece on stage has to include a range of performers rather than provide a vehicle for a 'star'. Company spirit and the desire to share something with an audience is what matters. Also it is helpful to create a sense of working collaboratively so that the children trust one another in terms of critical judgement. They can work in groups of three or four but with a group aim. The quality of the work is enhanced by careful work in small groups rather than a watered down programme for everyone. The deadlines mentioned earlier can help with this.

3 The performing arts need not be subject-bound but can be *truly interdisciplinary* reflecting a diversity of skills (maths may well be included in set design, science in lighting etc.), expressive form (dance-drama or music-theatre) and range of ability in the participants so that every skill is respected: the performer is equal to the writer, the carpenter to the designer. This element of respect between areas of responsibility was relected in an arts project involving 9 year olds. Throughout the project the children were allocated roles and it seemed that the actors were very important to the project. However, the prompter was a quiet child with reading difficulties. When the actors began to work without scripts and under more pressure, he became the person on whom they all relied. Having heard the play right through several times he became familiar with the script and more confident in his ability to read it. In the performance, what would in normal terms be considered a disaster when one actor forgot all his lines, became a triumph as the prompter coped so well with the situation. Similarly a child working as stage manager was equally effective. Everyone in the class could see

that the actors on the stage were performing better because they had a team of supporters providing back up.

4   *Any evaluation should be genuine.* Individual development is more important than a mark. (Many students can achieve a 'good' result without making any effort or progress at all. Other students progress enormously without achieving an obviously impressive end product. If we imagine a ten point scale, a child who has progressed from 2 to 7 has moved further than the child who has gone from 9 to 10, yet an onlooker will tend to judge the performance in terms of natural ability. It is very easy for talented musicians to underachieve because their work is of a comparatively high standard. To avoid this, the teacher can adopt a vocabulary of intelligent questioning, challenging assumptions so that the student can make his or her own decisions on value of the work. Adult beginner pianists often say that they want to play well enough to amuse themselves. The professional player, by contrast, never reaches such a goal. The terms of judgement need to be valid for the form: neatness is not an important factor in early design ideas but later accuracy is crucial. In writing for performance (as opposed to wall display) it is believability or the sound of a piece that is important.

5   Security is important too. The supportive teacher doesn't put a child 'on the spot' so that she needs to hold on to her position, but encourages self-criticism. In one class a pupil had composed a melody and the teacher could see that it could be improved by different instrumentation. He suggested other instruments which were tried out but, *having been through the processes* of trying out other sounds (and this is important) the child still preferred the original melody. At this point the teacher stepped down and accepted the decision in the knowledge that it was an informed one.

There is no right answer in the arts. It's very difficult to know why we like certain music or dance or why certain plays have been preserved. In script writing, children often assume that a teacher knows how a piece will start or end. In music composition it can be assumed that a particular outcome is desirable. Children can learn that there are many solutions to any one problem.

Real tasks

So what is a 'real' task?

It certainly isn't an exercise in a textbook. This is not to say that worksheets and project work are not valuable but they are primarily for enhancing skills and technique where necessary. A 'real' task has a purpose, a deadline and a natural outcome. The timescale is not important: a block of work lasting a week can be as valuable as one lasting three months if carefully planned. How often, for example, are children aware of having ended a project? An ending is not the end of a lesson, term or year .... It is the culmination of a series of events and challenges. With a performing arts project the tasks need to have a purpose at the outset which the children can be made aware of and recognise the achievement of it. They can be aware that they have progressed in terms of knowledge and skills. All the component parts of a project can then be seen in a helpful context.

There is usually a *sense of a puzzle or problem* (How can I do this? Can I use music here?)

A group of top juniors were working on a stage piece which involved an exploding computer. Paul was in charge of working out a way to make this work on stage. Over the course of several lunchtimes he and a group got together to solve the problem. There seemed to be no way to make the computer explode. Their search for a solution led them to ring local companies providing items for amateur theatre companies and a joke shop. One of these suggested a smoke-box which was not possible for safety reasons. However the idea of a smoke-box prompted the group to think in terms of lighting and eventually they came up with the idea of putting Paul inside the computer from where he could throw streamers while lights flickered on and off. Additionally a tape was made of the computer's song. Paul could start the tape-recorder from inside the computer. A mother who knew about stage lighting was brought in to advise. She assessed the capability of the simple stage lighting already in the school and took a small group of pupils through the process of placing the lights in different positions, sometimes lighting from the back of the stage, sometimes with lights in the front of the actors until the group was able, through practical experience, to achieve a black-out and flashing lights effects for the scene. It was clear to all the children involved that the answer to the problems came, not from their teachers, but from the children involved. There was a sense of achievement when they were solved.

At some point the pupil will feel *inadequate before the task* ('I will never do this'). Another group was working on some songs for a stage piece. At the beginning of the term the prospect of composing eight different songs seemed impossible to them but after several weeks of preliminary work they were able to compose very fast, put together a very adventurous score and found it necessary to discard material.

The child will realise *the need for guidance and help* ('I can't get the effect I need with these instruments'). When working on a piece of choreography a class wanted to create something totally different from anything else they had done. They wanted to differentiate between types of animals. Their own experience was in creative dance and they had been to a classical ballet. The teacher, however, invited a kathakali dancer to visit the school and work with him sparked off tremendous excitement. No one in the class had experienced classical Indian dance of this quality before and the children were enthralled by the explanations of the stories illustrated by the dancer such as 'Lord Krishna and the butler'. At the beginning of the demonstration the dancer explained some of the steps and how they built up to a narrative. Later, the children were able to learn simple steps and to incorporate them in their work. It is not always possible to provide such stimulus at will, but a school can build up a 'bank' of such resources using video, audio cassette, photographs, parents and professional artists in the neighbourhood. Often teachers know of local people who are happy to be involved in the life of the school on a voluntary basis.

There will be a *sense of triumph* ('I've done it!'). At the end of a project children will often say 'It was the best thing I've done'. There is no reason why this experience shouldn't be more frequent, with each project reaching higher levels than the one before.

Real skills

These are appropriate skills. This is not just handwriting for its own sake. Children need to see the importance of whatever skills they learn: writing words *for performance* and writing it legibly *so other children can read it* (or learning to use a word processor for the same task); performing a piece of music in a way that makes it *pleasurable for others to listen to;* making a costume that *will last until the final performance*. When there is an interchange between roles (the composer is not the performer, for example) this will make sense. A group of children writing letters to the local newspaper to tell them of a school event will need to include details of time, place and date and to make sure there is an address and telephone number on the letterhead. And the group gets a response.

A piece requires a rag-time effect? Introduce the idea of syncopation. If composers, for example, are working on music for lyrics, then simple tunes might not convey the appropriate atmosphere and specific technical skills might be useful (computer sounds or other compositional techniques).

The actors cannot remember when to come in? Introduce the concept of a stage manager. Often a group of players will ask if a teacher or pupil can act as a conductor when they see a need for it. Group composition will lead to this. The role of the conductor is then clear.

The actors are too slow? Take them through an exercise to solve the problem. One director working with children in a school set up a series of improvisation exercises. He took a section of script and concentrated on it for several minutes. First he asked the actors to read the script without actions with a special rule that each line had to start before the line before had finished. Then he asked the group to speak the lines in jibberish so that there was no problem over the actual words. Thirdly the children spoke the lines as slowly as possible, and then very fast. At the end of all these very enjoyable exercises the actors returned to the script refreshed and were able to perform more convincingly.

If the room doesn't suit the play, a group of children can produce a model box to try out effects.

Real achievement

There is a sense in which something valuable has been achieved when it is not a teacher who has given an arbitrary remark ('This work is quite good. Try the next exercise') but when there is an objective sense of success ('Class 1 liked it') and achievement ('I'd like to try this again, but next time...'). The child will not be afraid to be self-critical. Unlike a situation where a child feels the need to defend herself for pride's sake, within the safety of the project and within the environment created through the process of learning through experience, the pupil will actively seek out criticism and advice. There will be a sense of 'Does this work?', 'How could this be better?' 'How can this be developed?'

In summary any performing arts project should be relevant to the child *now*. It isn't just training for the future.

And if all this is achieved there will be noticeable signs of growth which can be examined against:

• the thought process
• the way a child looks at a problem

- the skills acquired
- the sense of achievement and motivation to continue
- analysis of the work of others.

Finally, of course, there is the need to seek out *role-models*; examples of good practice in other children, adults and professionals. Pupils then see that the activities in which they are participating are valued by others and practised by them. Take the example of football. From 8 or 9 years old, boys and, increasingly, girls take part in playing football games at school. There is usually a school team, a local team and regular television coverage at national and international level. On television there is detailed analysis of goals scored, good play and examples of adult players who have achieved success. Then there is the World Cup and coverage of the stars' lives in popular newspapers. Boys gain a serious interest in soccer from an early age and a respect for those who play it professionally. They take their own playing seriously. With the performing arts too there can be opportunities for people to see professional performances, so gaining an understanding of good practice and a respect for professional artists. Like young footballers, they will look at their own attempts in the light of what professionals achieve. It would be useful to identify similar role models in the arts and to be conscious of the impact of media coverage and 'hidden' statements made in conversations. There's a need to look at arts teaching through a child's eyes to consider inferences that could be made by the child. Do the children know adults who take the arts seriously? Are they aware of a relationship between what they do in school and professional practice?

Another interesting comparison with the football world is the problem of balancing the needs of 'potential professionals' against those of the whole group. Football managers sometimes argue that the very fact that boys and girls play 'proper' football from a young age can be damaging to their potential development as first class players. Youngsters, they argue, need to learn skills and technique first. This is also true of the performing arts, particularly in dance and instrumental work, where the 'showing of classroom work' is of far more value than trying to put on a full length 'production'. (Local papers sometimes carry stories of primary school Shakespeare productions!) Teachers can be aware of children with extraordinary talent but this can be balanced into an integrated arts policy that stretches all children.

The following chapters will take us through the stages of building up a performing arts programme in schools.

Notes

1   For a more detailed analysis of pre-service teacher training in the arts see *The arts, a preparation to teach* (Initial training for Primary teachers) by Shirley Cleave and Caroline Sharp NFER 1986.
2   Peter and Iona Opie: *Children's games in street and playground* and *Language and lore of schoolchildren*.

Another interesting reference book is *The arts in schools: Principles, practice and provision* published by the Calouste Gulbenkian Foundation, 1982.

HMI *Curriculum matters: The Curriculum from 5–16,* HMSO.

2 The child as communicator and creator

The performing arts are about communication. Most teachers realise the need to build on children's interests and experiences but often feel under pressure to deal with more obviously 'suitable' classroom topics (like 'The Romans'). When asked what concerns them, even young children will come up with very immmediate issues: attitudes to peers, parents, adults, conflicts in the playground, school, home. And yet it is only when there is open discussion about issues of concern that any realisation of how to deal with the world, and with others can be established.

Similarly with music and dance, it is not necessary to obstruct creative ideas with conventional ideas about harmony or counterpoint in music or dance technique. These things come later (and will be discussed more fully in Chapter 3 *The Child as Interpreter and Performer*). First of all one needs to draw out ideas from the individual or the group. Ideas can take many forms. The skill of deciding how best to express something is a vital one. To illustrate this point, consider how a similar story can be treated differently in dance, theatre and music. The use of music to create emotional atmosphere is extremely clear, for example, in Puccini's work. In *La Bohème* the music reminds the audience of past episodes in the lovers' lives. In *Madama Butterfly* a humming chorus evokes a mood which is reminiscent of a previous emotion-filled scene. Classical ballet can suggest, for example, vulnerability in movement by its use of the body. Straight theatre, on the other hand, can be flexible in the hands of the interpreters (directors and actors). Contrast the amount of freedom an actor has to interpret his or her lines (timing, emphasis, tone, accent) with a singer who is at the mercy of the notes and conductor's tempo.

Children too can use the different qualities of sound or movement to convey emotions. When trying to convey a nightmare about a central character's parents' divorce, a group of top juniors hit on the idea of a hijack as a metaphor for his state of mind. They wanted to put over the point that the boy's life was falling in around him and that there was no way in which he could cope with the pressures closing in on him. At the time of the project there were one or two hijack stories in the press and this analogy seemed to fit very well. The sequence was set in the boy's bedroom where he was first seen tossing in his bed obviously unable to sleep. As the music began, other characters appeared behind the boy to sing the central song about the hijack. As the song progressed they turned into terrorists with guns and throughout the song the boy continued to toss and turn. The lighting flickered in line with the volume as in a disco and the song itself 'exploded' in the chorus of 'This is a hijack' with different characters echoing 'hijack'. The piece built up into a very explosive number aptly reflecting the idea of the piece. Thus the children were able to use drama, music and three simple free-standing lights with dimmers attached, to maximum effect and to use what is generally thought of as a rather sophisticated idea, that of metaphor.

Writing, drawing, music-making, dancing can, of course, occur for their own sakes. It is possible to choreograph a piece about the nature of dance and explore or glorify particular steps or, in music, specific techniques. This is valid and worth exploring. Another way of beginning a performing arts project is to begin with an issue or interest and work from there.

It is essential to get the creative process going: the more ideas there are, the more material there is to work with. If there are plenty of ideas in music, dance or words, this 'bank' of ideas is certain to contain some very good material. If, on the other hand, there is a struggle to find one idea, then the likelihood of it being a good one is lower. The aim is to enable all the pupils to be 'creative', as well as to nurture creative ability in the obviously talented. If the teacher encourages 'instinctive creativity' ie. he or she encourages children to go to a keyboard and 'just compose', or to a space and 'dance', only a small group of people with natural skill and confidence will be able to achieve something. The rest will either get a very negative sense of their own abilities or discount the activity completely. This is not to invalidate 'improvisation' as an approach, as ideally improvisation is a total approcah built up over a long period of time, and totally dependent on the skill of the teacher to take the pupil on. A good teacher of music, for example, will have a careful plan of classroom work that builds up over many sessions. Children will begin with very strict guidelines: using only 4 notes, for example, and the teacher will respond to each pupil or group, suggesting ways to develop, music to listen to and instrumentation, over many months. A music post holder can often work in this way, picking out interesting ideas in the pupils' work and using them as a springboard for new projects.

Remember that any teacher can find two or three paintings from a class, worthy of wall display. It takes more skill to structure an art class so that all the children's work is worthy of display, showing that each child has progressed in his or her own individual terms and can take pride in what has been achieved. If work can be organised in this way, the chances are, there is a safe environment for creative work and a space where children can feel happy to express themselves and can work at their material.

Finding a subject for writing

At one time it was the fashion in art lessons to give pupils 'subjects' for their 'art'. One week it would be 'the seaside', another 'a winter scene' and so on. Alternatively a term's work might centre on a medium or a technique e.g. pastels or tie dye. These are useful starting points from which the pupil concerned can develop an interest in a particular medium or subject (as professional artists do, for example David Hockney's swimming pools).

Finding a subject matter for a performing arts piece to be worked at by a group is more difficult. There will, however, be subject areas that motivate a group and by bringing them to the surface the group will 'gel' in a co-operative and non-competitive fashion. One way to begin is to ask individuals 'What concerns you?'. This is better done anonymously, written on paper perhaps. Pupils usually suggest topics such as:

- my family: relationships between parents and children, expectations of parents, what is home? anxieties about parents, death in the family, siblings.
- friends: why they are important, what makes a friend?
- animals: emotional ties with pets, losing pets, when pets die.
- school: achievements, expectations, relationships with teachers, friends, others at school.

Bigger issues such as racism or the way girls are treated also concern children, although these are seldom expressed as 'isms'. Children perceive such things, quite rightly, as they affect those around them. Such issues can be tackled 'head on' if they come up.

It is often surprising how 'adult' the thinking about such subjects is. It is true, of course, that when it comes down to daily living, children react in just the same way as adults. Children are as deeply affected by divorce, death, stress in the family as adults are, and when offered an opportunity to discuss such things they will open up. Although children seem to understand quite early on that adults don't expect them to discuss such things!

In discussion it will become evident that some of these themes are of general interest or, in some sense are 'of the moment'. It is possible to react to these by saying 'The ideas were too juvenile' or 'There wasn't enough in them to work into a project'; often the teacher has already planned a topic like 'the Normans' or 'the human body'. Children who have been questioned about what they think, however, will often respond to a project far more positively if it starts where they are and will say 'No one ever asked us before'. There is no harm in developing the theme along a particular route at a later date. Indeed to start a project on 'Victorian Britain' with pertinent and relevant questions about life today is a most appropriate way of encouraging an interest in an earlier period. Such questions as 'What interests you?', 'What do you care about?' can be developed into what Victorian children cared about: attitudes to parents and family, work and school.

Consider a topic such as 'my family'. Think about aspects of the topic: parents, grandparents, brothers and sisters, my house, my road, the shops, my pets. How easy it is to extend the aspects. For example, my parents' home, their parents' home, conditions, income, expenditure, children's health, lifestyle (school, leisure) and so on. By taking on what might be termed 'commonplaces' a route into more 'extended' topic work can be secured.

It is simple to develop the theme into a statement: What concerns children about 'the family' or 'school'? Statements that have come out of children's ideas have been:

Family: **My parents care more about their work than they do about me.** Again such a theme can be developed.

- Why do adults care about material needs?
- What are our basic needs, (homes, food, clothing)?
- Where do these come from?
- How much do they cost?
- Family income.
- Problems of 'making ends meet'.
- Work.

Friends: **Our attitudes to friends often change and we have to adapt our feelings.** (9-year-old)

Feelings: **Everyone has feelings but we often treat some**

people as if they had no feelings. (11-year-old)

Ourselves: **White children assume that all black children in Africa are starving.** (11-year-old)

With such subjects to deal with, it is possible to create music and dance straightaway. Or, if preferred, you can go back to Chapter 1 and work out characters who can react in certain improvised situations. To do this, one would ask individuals to create characters and to imagine the characters in specific roles. In the 'Feelings' example above a plot was created around an original science fiction story. It centred around a group of children playing in a science museum. One boy pressed a button which took the rocket they were exploring into space. They landed on another planet inhabited by Ancientos. The Ancientos were serviced by a group of inferior creatures called Antronics. During the course of their stay the children came to realise that the Antronics had feelings and were suffering badly at the hands of the Ancientos who, assuming that they had no feelings, kicked and bullied them. A crisis occured and the Antronics risked their lives in order to save the planet and the children were able to point out to the Ancientos the courage of the Antronics. The plot became quite a complex one but the theme and statement of the piece were fairly simple. The three types of creature: Human, Anciento and Antronic enabled the teacher to ask different groups to compose different types of music for each one. The two environments: earth and the planet needed different atmospheres. The language the three groups used helped the audience to differentiate between them. In fact the Antronics 'spoke' on a monotone (a sort of recitative). Musically and visually there were interesting possiblities: a duet between an Antronic and an Anciento or a Human required two musical styles coming together.

It is clear how such material, perfect for drama treatment, feeds into all aspects of the primary school curriculum. Some of the subjects mentioned above, form useful starting points for discussion in class assembly or as part of the RE or moral curriculum. Another example dealt with the subject of disability and what it is like to be wheelchair-bound. In such a case the teacher can organise opportunities for the children to carry out research. A group of children could ask local organisations for information about facilities for the disabled. In one school a group borrowed a wheelchair and went out (supervised) to the local shops where they could see the problems of not being able to reach lift buttons, access to toilets and restaurants and could experience first hand how people often talk to or across people in wheelchairs. In the earlier example of 'Granny's dead', discussion about attitudes to the elderly, ideas about death and social behaviour between peers provided several opportunities for discussion about moral issues. Background research makes for believable characters in a play or story. Even ordinary story telling is enhanced by experience of real life.

Having amassed such material the most important lesson any 'creative' person has to learn is how to discard material. Everyone knows that the more one does something the more skilled one becomes. When, however, we try to get children to produce something 'creative', we tend to think in terms of one try only. Have you ever been in a situation, for example, when in order to stimulate creative writing you have simply written some titles on the board and then expected results? Having received the written work, the lesson is over, the 'creativity' produced and the next lesson can move to new subject matter and any problems encountered have not been tackled. An alternative approach is to encourage redrafting. Obviously it is tedious to constantly rewrite but there are ways of structuring writing so that re-drafting is not merely correcting. Editing work can suggest a natural need for introducing a word-processor into the classroom. This also enables a child, working on writing to be shared, to produce an attractive piece of work for distribution. Improvisation can also help and spending time to work out ideas before going to the page is the most valuable of all. In fact it can be very helpful to actively discourage writing ideas down in full too soon. In the case of 'The Anciento Enigma' discussed above, the children went through a very detailed preparation process for the writing long before anything was written.

Some of the children involved, described the process in a special book about the project:

> **We made a big chart of the things we cared about. We then chose the most popular emotions and decided on a describing word which would tie them all together. We decided on caring. Our next job was to create the characters. There were going to be 12 characters as this number was easy to work with. We put up 12 large sheets of paper around the room and thought of describing words for each character.**

They worked out all the characters in a group and made notes of their qualities and weaknesses on the large sheets of paper. Then the characters were examined in terms of how they would 'get on with' other characters. This involved several discussion sessions with the teacher asking such questions as 'How would character A get on with character B?' and 'Why?'. The children could then work out certain scenes on their feet. The characters could be given names and could be played by different children. An example might be the first scene on the planet. The teacher would say 'Imagine you are an Anciento meeting the children for the first time. How would you react?' Once they had tried to act out such a scene it could be discussed and different children would have different opinions. Eventually when the group was pleased with a scene they could write it down or tape it, to be typed out and distributed later. The school had a word-processor and the children used it to work out the script. This meant that subtle changes could be made easily, at any stage.

The children prepared a summary of each scene. Here is their description of Scene 2.

Scene 2: The planet

They (the children) **land on the planet and are met by Mary, a human who had been sent into space. Mary takes them to the village where they witness cruelty by the planet people, the Ancientos. The Ancientos tell the children that they need special food for their survival. A force-field had developed around the food, so they built the Antronics, which are made of metal, to travel through the force-field to fetch food.**

The summary provided the foundation for this dialogue.

HELEN **Are these real animals?**

MARY **No, they're mechanical**

JOHN **What is this Seyogo that we heard them talking about?**

MARY **It's a special mineral needed in their diet for their survival**

HELEN **Why can't they get it themselves?**

MARY **Many years ago a one way force-field developed around the only location on the planet where the mineral supply would grow. Because they could not enter this zone it was necessary to build Antronics which would be programmed to travel through and bring back the mineral needs for the Ancientos.**

Discussion and experiments about magnetism in science project work complemented the arts project: students found out about the properties of magnets and their uses in modern living: from fridge magnets to complicated industrial machinery. This ensured careful research for the arts project and interest by the group in expanding the project beyond the arts.

Children bring to the classroom their personal histories to date. Each child in the group has a personal past that begins with birth and a family history including special events, culture and experience. Within a classroom there is an enormous fund of such resources. In any one class there might be different religious groupings or it could be a very closed community where everyone shares similar circumstances. Out of such experiences, creativity can grow. Imagine, for example, creating a piece of theatre about 'Family festivals'. In some classrooms it would be possible to research festivals of different origins and present them to other classes. The children themselves might be able to find out information on festivals and ceremonies by asking their parents or grandparents or going to the library. For example, what happens at:

* a christening?
* Purim?
* Divali?

When all the relevant information has been gathered, short sketches could be performed. Children from schools where there is total or near total representation from one cultural or social group should still be encouraged to explore material and experiences of other groups.

If we look in detail at some of these experiences of everyday life we can find starting points and can compile 'banks' of tunes, stories, rhymes, ideas.

Ask any group of children about the following.

1   *religious stories, myths and folktales*: we have mentioned ceremonies, many of which, like Purim, grow out of religious stories. Often such stories have a moral, or theme, common to many cultural groups. Others are peculiar to one source. Such stories provide springboards. The story does not have to have an extended narrative. It could be, perhaps, the story of the tables in Heaven and Hell, each with a large bowl piled high with rice. In Heaven the people were happy and contented while in Hell they were starving and cross. The reason for the difference was contained in the attitudes of the people themselves. In Hell they were forced to eat the rice with extremely long chopsticks and dropped the rice from the chopsticks when trying to eat. In Heaven, by contrast, they helped one another to rice across the table and so all lived in happy contentment. A story like this can be told in seconds, it's really very short, but in drama terms it

could have potential. Elaborate stories are best told as stories, but simple tales or morals can be enhanced by music, dance and drama and made into a performing arts piece. Structures are important. In this instance the piece can be presented as two contrasting scenes, with one group working on Hell and the other Heaven. The music for each scene will be different in rhythm and instrumentation (whereas perhaps the melody could be the same for both). Dance groups can prepare contrasting movement ideas. The two scenes could be linked by a narrator.

2   *poems and rhymes*: the Opies' work is helpful here, but it can be helpful to gather and catalogue rhymes and poems known by the children themselves plus, of course, any that they have invented. This has the bonus of privileging the children's own knowledge over ideas from books. Often music composition relating to a mood (e.g. as above 'mood music for hell') can be extended by a theme from a piece of poetry (perhaps, for the above, an original piece written by a child on the subject of 'greed'). It helps a poet to have an 'atmosphere' already created, and a poem, in turn might stimulate more musical themes.

3   *playground chants*: there are often newly invented or re-worked versions of these which can be discussed.

4   *tunes and songs*: as well as 'traditional' material there are the many tunes and songs from the pop world that will be known to whole classes of children. It is, of course, ironic that there is so little music listening and music making in schools when children spend so much of their leisure time enjoying music!

5   *dance steps*: again there are fashions in movement (such as break-dancing and tap) that can be incorporated in classroom choreography and so give status to those pupils who have skill in these areas. Also more traditional movement e.g. hopscotch or skipping can be worked into a piece. Good dance can spring out of 'life' and if narrative is attempted, these aspects of movement can be integrated with tremendous effect.

These are starting points and should not be confused with entire projects. It's easy to start at the same spot *always* and not to progress at all! This is where the skilled teacher will add something: offer books to read, suggest ideas, widen experiences with visits, visitors, schools broadcasts and music.

A pool of ideas

'Banks' of ideas (tunes and moods in music, for example) amassed over a period of time can be organised later on. In getting the ideas, virtually any method is valid. It is important, however, to clear the mind of preconceptions. Don't try, in music, for example, to write in the style of a particular composer, pop or classical. Such writing will always be derivative and the best will be less good than the composer intended. Sophisticated instruments can inhibit compositional work, for example extensive use of sets of electronic keyboards limit variety of composition and use only the keyboard skills available in the class. Most pupils will be aware from television of what is possible on these instruments and will, therefore, feel frustrated by their own attempts at composition. Using groups of students playing a variety of simple percussion is often more interesting.

Composing melodies

As we have said, everyone comes to the composing process with a background, personal history and cultural experience which will include music. In composing with children it is important to use these as a starting point. It is very easy for those of us with some music training to fall back on traditional harmony and counterpoint, thus forcing children into musical theory. In the primary school it is more helpful to have an open mind in terms of what can be achieved, rather than feeling that what children compose has to be restricted to what can be notated or what the teacher might feel happy with. If there is a need for notation it can be done in any way that can be 'read' back.

Tunes are a very accessible starting point. There is no right way to compose them nor any correct method of assessment. What we enjoy in terms of a tune or vocal line is largely a matter of taste and/or what works. Although it is clearly possible to analyse music in terms of harmony, this doesn't really help in dealing with composition with young children. In primary schools, just as with painting, composing comes first and theory, if at all in the primary years, later. The chief thing is to generate material by whatever way possible. The key is to find a method which can grow with the children and is not self-limiting as composing in the style of another composer can be. Specialist music teachers will be keen to use improvisation techniques but for teachers without a musical background, starting from the shape provided by a pattern is an effective method.

In a series of projects for the Education department of the Royal Opera House, composer Edward Lambert evolved a way of working with young children of all abilities. Children were asked to compose their own individual tunes on tuned percussion. First of all they were asked to make up number patterns using four numbers only. This was quite enjoyable as the children could devise quite long and complicated patterns.

1234
4343
2421
3241

Others came up with more complex patterns such as

1
12
222
1212
21331

Each number was then attached to a note on a xylophone or glockenspiel. The simple 'tune' above became (without any rhythm):

The composers could then experiment with rhythm and with repeating notes.

Merely establishing a code of this type will ensure that the piece builds up a familiar pattern with the listener and will, if used effectively, be enjoyable and acceptable listening.

Individuals and groups can amass any number of such tunes in this manner. They can play them at different speeds, with different rhythms, on different instruments. They can play them backwards, or start in the middle.

Thus we might have a second tune (the first tune backwards):

Phrases within the bigger phrase can be repeated:

These phrases can form a new section and then another phrase can be played forwards and backwards:

Then perhaps the sections could be combined:

Although the teacher might prefer to use conventional notation there is really no need for it at this stage as the purpose of any notation will be for the children themselves who might prefer to develop their own system of notation.

1 = C	1 4 23 1 / 24234 /
2 = D	3 44 3 / 2 1 1 //
3 = E	
4 = F	

At any point, using this method, the tune can be changed, lengthened or shortened and adjusted to suit taste or needs (possibly in terms of a script). It should be emphasised that such ideas do not conform to traditional harmony-type music teaching. Even adding conventional rhythms as has been done here for the purpose of giving examples, is misleading. This is simply a way of generating melodies or tunes. The students themselves will determine whether or not the tunes are acceptable or whether they need to be altered in terms of rhythm or notes. In fact the children will tend to want complicated rhythms that the non-music specialist will not be able to notate conventionally. It's quite common for the composers to set the players quite difficult performing tasks e.g. two players working in different time signatures. This is fine as it sets up a new problem: the children themselves need to notate their melody in whatever way they can! Sometimes the teacher *can't* do it for them. This also engages children in the need to invent their own symbolism which reflects what they want to communicate to their peers. This links with other symbolic languages including mathematics.

Words can be set to melodies written in this way.

Give the composers the words to be set and a melody already composed and ask them to fit the two together by adding notes, changing the length of notes or the rhythm as appropriate.

Clouds in the sky
The sun up high
And what a pleasant day it is
Jump out of bed
Ready to play.

This pattern system can be used to make 'mood music' too, used to create a setting. Pupils can explore different sounding instruments and try various types of mood, for example, mystery, a storm or a party. They can also experiment with the speed of the piece, using silence and change of tempo and can vary rhythm. A simple exercise would be to give each group of children a word or idea (such as seasons or feelings) and ask each one to compose an appropriate piece of music. When the pieces are played back to the class the other children can comment on their effectiveness. Ideally a group works together to compose for a number of instruments rather than composing a tune and then arranging it in the conventional way. 'Arranging' in the sense of writing a melody and then orchestrating it, requires technical know-how that is unnecessary at this point but it is very valuable to compose for large forces. A tambourine, for example, might only play in very tiny sections throughout a piece but could add something of importance. An 'arranger' would need a good deal of experience to add a tambourine part to a tune afterwards.

Rather than compose a tune you can compose a whole piece for several instruments. First construct an arbitrary pattern using a number for every member of the group (in this case a group of four). In this instance the number pattern becomes the *score*, not the melody as in the previous example. The purpose of the score in this example is to give the players a patterned order of playing.

We could start with the song 'composed' above. This could be the tune we wish to set and a 'mood' for the piece could be established, say cheerful. Four instruments can be selected with the mood in mind. Ideally this would be two pitched instruments (perhaps a xylophone and some chime bars) and two unpitched (a drum and triangle). The score is created in the same way as before:

4234
3342
1141
3331
1342
1221

The pattern represents the order of playing. The melody can be played and the players can 'improvise' in the given order so that the group comes up with a piece that they are happy with. The numbers can represents bars, part-bars or longer moments of music. Also the numbers can be of different lengths. If a melody is used, the 'score' should start before it begins in order to give an introduction.

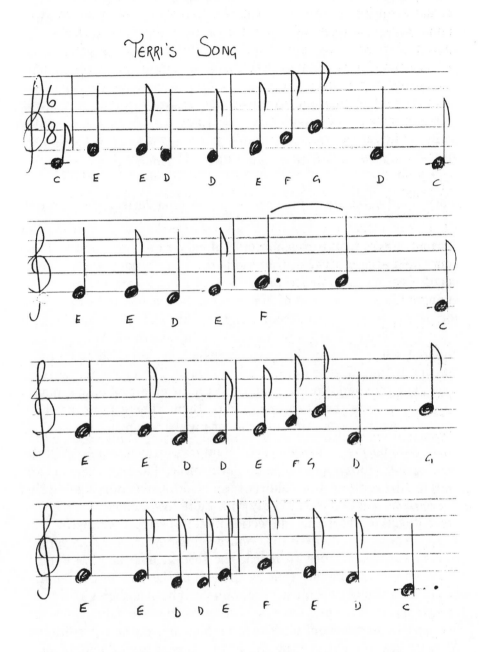

Figure 1 *Child composers can create their melodies in any way. The teacher can then notate them in whatever way the players can understand.*

Each member of the group can either pick out a motif from the existing melody or choose to echo a small fragment of it. Alternatively the player can compose a new figure, motif or rhythm to be played in the order constructed. One player might need to point to the number in order to bring the group members in. The group can try playing the 'composition' horizontally (42343342 etc.) or vertically (431311,231332 etc.). While experimenting the group can be encouraged to try as many ideas as possible but as soon as they like a particular section they can record it in some way. If, for example, the introduction is felt to be good then the group can go on to the next line.

They could make any number of compositional decisions within the pattern.

Player 3 might play throughout and alone on his/her number. This could be a simple rhythm that holds the piece together. The order could change at certain points, the speed for a certain line could change. Thus a great deal of material can be created and this allows for decisions about what material to keep, what to abandon and what to develop. There are no rules in this method! At any point children can abandon the method, which is intended only as a starting point. As a technical exercise the pupils might try to take their four numbers 'to the limit' and try to investigate how many musical patterns they can create with them. There is no need to stick to four numbers; any amount of numbers can be selected.

When composing a piece called 'Bonfire party' a group of girls worked out a formula as above for their piece. The piece was in two sections. In the first the bonfire was lit and it slowly got going. In the second half there was a party with more lively music. One of the group suggested that the 1st section should be repeated at the end to create an atmosphere of the bonfire dying down. Everyone agreed that it was a good idea to repeat the section but there was some discussion about the fact that by the end of the section the bonfire had built up and the music was quite lively. Another girl in the group suggested playing the first section backwards ending with the first sparks of the bonfire. The girls had arrived at a traditional ABA musical piece. Once the ability to compose 'tunes' and 'moods' at will is achieved material can be amassed for any purpose.

When composing in this way each group should be encouraged to share their composition with the rest of the class. If several groups are composing in this way the teacher can ask simple critical questions:

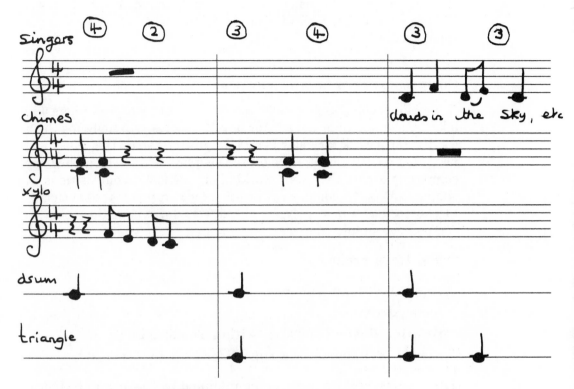

- how was the piece composed?
- what made it sound eerie? (or any other mood)
- Is it altered by playing it on different instruments? (try alto xylophone, piano, clarinet, voice or untuned percussion)
- could the rhythm be altered?
- could the speed be changed?
- would making it louder or softer affect how it is heard?
- if an emotion is required (e.g. anger) can it be conveyed in different ways? Can anger be loud and soft?
- what happens when a group of instruments play the tune in unison?
- how was the piece structured?

Music of this 'atmospheric' type can be used as programme music to illustrate children's prose, poetry or painting. Also it can be used for drama and dance. With both moods and tunes, ideas can be remembered and stored in a mood music 'bank' or 'tunebank' and can be called out for future use. Ultimately several sections of music can be joined into a long piece or can be linked by a narrative. A particular idea might fit into a larger piece. If a group were writing music to illustrate a conflict between two characters, they could use two 'tunes' from the bank against a background of mood music. There's no need for the two characters' 'tunes' to be written at the same time.

Composing for others to perform

Professional composers usually take account of their performers and adapt music for their benefit (or develop scores especially for them e.g. Britten's work for Peter Pears). Pupils too can do this. They will need to find out about the voices and players for which they are composing before they start working on particular compositions. A simple exercise in composing for others would be for the musicians to choose a group of players and singers for whom they plan to compose. A simple chart can be compiled.

Mai-Lin's group

JENNY: **recorder (can play g,a,b,c,d)**

SIMON: **drum**

ROBERTO: **singer (can sing within range c-b)**

DARREN: **xylophone (we can choose up to 5 notes)**

The composing team need not be inhibited by the lack of technical skill of their performers.

It is likely in a primary school that there will be several beginner recorder players who can only play these notes:

If this is the case then the composers should have started out with their tunes with this limitation. There is still plenty of scope here!

It could also be, of course, that some players in this group can play these notes with different degrees of expertise so that, for example, one player could only play these notes in order up and down while another can move quite happily between the notes. This is a further limitation but can easily be accommodated:

PLAYER 1

PLAYER 2

Composing for a singer or group of singers can be done in another way. The methods outlined above could throw up unsingable melodies (or rather melodies requiring expertise in a singer). If a melody is intended to be sung it is better to work with a group of singers direct.

A group of boys working on a version of a West Indian Ananse story were trying to set the following verse created by a group of writers.

It is daytime again

I have to rise and go

Once more again to work

What a life, what a life.

The boys tackled the task first by reading through the lines as a chant and soon came up with an agreed tempo and rhythm. One by one they chanted the line and then tried to sing it.

They settled on:

Sounds with words

Figure 2   *This song was performed as an unaccompanied round (like the popular song 'London's burning'). The result was a haunting chant that contrasted Chima's loneliness with Charmaine's anger.*

Sounds can work with words or against them. Often when adding sounds to dialogue, what is being said is emphasised, for example by adding suspense music when something exciting is going to happen. Also music can be used to comment either positively or ironically. For example in opera a singer can make a statement that the audience can read ironically because of a particular motif in the orchestra. In Britten's opera *Peter Grimes*, for example, a simple courtyard scene is set to music in such a way that the audience is clear with which characters it should sympathise. The coroner and 'accused' are given standard things to say:

CORONER   Peter Grimes, take the oath after me. 'I swear by Almighty God'

PETER   'I swear by Almighty God . . .'

but by the musical setting at this point our sympathies go with Grimes. In children's work often a character will be singing happy words but the music will indicate sadness or fear.

Also, of course, sounds can operate in their own right, quite separately from words or dialogue. In Puccini's opera *La Bohème* there is a quartet in which two of the characters are quarelling, while the other two are making up. The accompaniment works for both pairs. Maybe the music is saying that breaking up and making up are parallel emotions?

Dance

Ideas in dance can be built up in exactly the same way. Units can be collected and can include:

- shapes: spiky shapes, angry shapes, curled shapes, long shapes
- movement themes: going from shape to shape, sequences of movements
- moving to music: watery movement, angry music
- moods: turbulent water, earthquakes, menace

These can then be stored (notated, videoed or even just remembered). Such ideas can be brought together for a joint composition which can be performed alongside the music. We should also remember that divisions between art-forms are arbitrary and should not be adhered to strictly in the primary school. It is helpful for the subject areas to overlap. An example would be to let a dance group lead the musicians. A dance piece can be put together within a simple structure (beginning, middle and end) on a particular theme. This can then be 'performed' to the music group who can then go away and compose for the dance. This breaks down the traditional view that it is necessary to start with a piece of music for choreography.

Acting and dance are complex forms requiring skills. It has been common amongst artists working in schools, or in 'outreach' or community work to present their art to 'the people' as if everybody given a workshop experience can immediately act, or dance or make music. While this is encouraging, to be truly effective, skills need to be acquired and this takes time.

As with composition, structures are vital to dance. Movement can be constructed *from the pupils' own ideas* in exactly the same way as the musical ones above. Small fragments, movements representing characters, or moods, or shapes are gathered together into a wider structure. This can then be made into a worthwhile and exciting piece with either freely composed music, or existing score. Dance work in the primary school mentioned above in connection with *Peter Grimes* involved the children in working on their own movements for the different sea interludes. Just as in the opera the children created their own characters during the Dawn music and built this up to create a danced scene with fishermen, traders, people walking by, until a whole danced scene was created. The piece came together as a total stage picture so that the entrances and exits were timed as the characters crossed the stage. The piece was easily structured because the piece of music limited it in terms of length. The whole scene was videoed so that the children could see how their individual character built in to the whole scene.

Organising ideas

A key to working either individually or as a group, is structure. Structure is a liberating force in any creative activity and allows a piece to be brought together as a totality for presentation. If a structure is imposed then the constraints are enabling. Also an overall structure can simplify organisation and make presentation more professional. At the outset of a project, for example, it can be decided that there will be two danced sections in a musical piece. If a longer piece of music-drama is being created this gives the chance to state quite clearly that within the piece are moods, emotions, feelings that cannot be communicated through words but are to be choreographed. The composing group will have the task to compose two sections specifically to be danced with the sections containing a certain amount of structure in their own right. These can be passed to the choreographic group. Similarly it can be decided that a major moment in the piece will be a large chorus piece with music and words for a large group of performers.

The idea of 'banks' of fragments for compilation at a later date is useful for many reasons. Firstly it utilises the early work done by pupils in a helpful way. Often an excellent idea comes up at the beginning of a project and is lost as the project progresses. If the ideas are 'banked' they can be developed later if there's a point where little progress is being made. Also they provide a framework and sense of achievement so that pupils can look back over a term or a few weeks and see where they have come from. They can appreciate that they have moved on in composition or dance and this brings confidence and eagerness to continue. Also where 'better' ideas have emerged the child can look back and discard earlier material of his or her own accord without having the ideas 'crossed out' by the teacher.

If you wanted to compose an 'overture' you would need to collect the ideas into a structure with sections:

Section A: setting the scene — a group of characters

Section B: development of *A* — conflict between the characters
Section C: resolution — the characters re-group

The possibilities for dividing into sections are infinite. Each major section above can, in its turn, be sub-divided so that each has a beginning, middle and end. Musical ideas can be intensified at different times in the piece, or worked on humorously or ironically.

If, at the same time, another group of children were working on a mime or dance with the same three part structure they could feed ideas to the musicians. For example, 'we need a silence at this point' or 'the conflict needs to be more intense here'.

What is important is to find starting points. Once these are in place the children can develop with or away from the original 'tune' which is really unimportant and merely serves as a 'way in'.

Not only can work be brought together within a class but a presentation across the school can be worked out thus enabling younger children to present their ideas alongside older children.

An example of such a project was *The seasons in Ongle*. Five classes of children worked on the creation of a piece of dance drama over several weeks.

Initially a group from four of the classes worked on the writing. Each class was given a theme: fire, water, earth and air. Each group researched their element and found out things that happen in each place e.g. earthquakes in the earth, kite-flying in the air. With a writer, they evolved a bank of ideas.

Fire: dragon of fire, wood of flames, three evil creatures travel through the fires
Water: putting out a fire, playing in water, swimming, heavy rainfall
Earth: farming and harvest, earthquake, rebuilding the land
Air: fresh and fragrant breeze, rainbow, kite-flying, washing and hanging out clothes

Across the classes a summary of the story emerged:

The story is of the farmers of Ongle who plant seeds and harvest the crops successfully. The Ongle countryside becomes lush and green.

One day there is a sudden and unexpected earthquake. The people are distraught but rebuild the land.

Jealousy, Greed and Hatred stalk the land. They leave Ongle and travel many miles to some nearby caves in

search of a dragon who might help them wage war against the people. When they reach the outskirts of the caves they encounter woods of fire through which they walk to the dragon.

Jealousy, Greed and Hatred face the dragon with their weapons and at last capture him by casting spells to force him to sleep.

Water spirits put out the fire left by the dragon. After heavy rainfall a rainbow appears in the sky and the people rejoice at the prospect of better days ahead.

Days after the rain a breeze of fresh and fragrant air sweeps the land enabling the people to wash their clothes and dry them in the courtyards. The people of Ongle celebrate the kite-flying festival. The best kites are left in the air as a symbolic gift to Mother Nature.

A composer organised the story so that each class could work on a section.

1A   Musical introduction
1B   Dance: The people of Ongle celebrate the harvest and are hit by an earthquake.
2A   Musical interlude
2B   Dance: Greed, Hatred and Jeolousy take on the dragon of fire.
3A   Musical interlude: The fire is put out.
3B   Dance: The rain refreshes the land and a rainbow appears.
4A   Musical interlude: A breeze of fresh air fills the land.
4B   Dance: The people celebrate the kite flying festival.
5   Finale

Simultaneously a group of dancers worked on their own movement ideas which were incorporated into a choreographed section. The sections were linked by compositions by a fifth class.

The right form

As mentioned in Chapter 1, reading and writing are not the only ways of learning and communicating. Restricting the performing arts only to words is to ignore other effective means which might be more appealing to some children.

The very best examples of works in any art-form are enhanced by the choice of form itself. For example synopses of ballets, operas and plays are often very complicated to read when the piece itself is often very accessible. This is usually because the form helps the piece along because it is as integral to the piece as the story. *Swan Lake*, for example, is not so much a story that is danced but a ballet that can, if necessary, be expressed as a story. If *Swan Lake* could be expressed only in words then it would be pointless to dance it. There are examples, of course, where a piece is not suited to the form chosen for it by its interpreter. It is interesting to compare those 'stories' treated in different art-forms. Usually there are examples within the pieces where a particular form works best. These make excellent points of departure with older primary school students. If stories have been used by several interpreters, like Shakespeare's *A Midsummer Night's Dream*, it is usually interesting material. Children, too, can compose, choreograph and create drama for such stories and then look at extracts from the existing versions. It is not always necessary to write a story for drama, music or dance treatment. Existing stories can be used. This leads on to the idea of recording work for performance purposes and performing it.

3 The child as interpreter and performer

There is a difference between creation and performing. Composers, writers and choreographers are not necessarily the best people to perform their own work and if they do so they limit their own creative abilities to the level of their own technical expertise and/or solo performance. Secondly, recording ideas makes them more permanent, 're-accessible' and gives them status. Also it can assist evaluation. Given the creative idea the skilled performer can greatly enrich it with his or her interpretation.

There is no need to think in terms of conventional notation or script unless you want to. Conventions of this type have evolved over a long period and are often quite difficult when dealing with recently created material. Contemporary professional composers, for example, often adapt conventional music notation for their own purposes because it is simply too limiting in terms of new writing. Video recording is now important in dance, and photography can also be useful and provides an opportunity for students to use the need to record in a 'creative' way. When talking about 'writing' in this context it is a very loose term for putting a script together. 'Writing' in this sense can mean improvisation or discussion. This sort of 'writing' might not be written down when the material is created. Ideas can be taken down by a pupil scribe during rehearsals. Here are some possibilities:

1 Each improvisation session can culminate in a final run-through with a tape-recorder or video. The teacher can transcribe material and have copies made.
2 Children can 'write' around a typewriter with the teacher or a pupil taking down ideas.
3 Children can work in groups around a word-processor. This allows considerable flexibility for editing. Each new session can start with the children reviewing the work from earlier sessions and adding new material.

It can be frustrating if notation is only for the purpose of record-keeping. [Notation and recording of this type need to have a purpose.] Apparently pointless struggles with theory will rarely succeed. Working on traditional theory with young children will tend to limit their creative work. In order to work 'accurately' they would need to start with theory. Writing is then restricted to what they can write (in terms of spelling and grammar) or compose (musical style will be limited to simple harmony) and their minds will be closed to wider possibilities. Children will often combine complex rhythms and moods quite naturally in a way which would seem too complex if working from traditional notation.

Creators themselves can take responsibility for passing their ideas on. Notation is most important when the composer is absent. The performer(s) can have an input into the piece and the piece can develop from this input. Let's look at an example of a music project when composing and performing were clearly distinguished. A composer worked over a period of weeks with a class. First he worked with a group of ten pupils who he called 'composers' even though they had no previous experience of music composition. They were all beginning to learn to play musical instruments and some had taken Grade 1 Associated Board examinations. This group began work on elementary composition ideas, composing melodies and moods. After this preliminary work they began to compose a dance score. The piece was divided into sections: beginning, middle and end and loosely given subject matter.

Section 1: setting the scene
Section 2: conflicts
Section 3: resolution

At no point was there a blow by blow account of the narrative, and much emerged later with a choreographer. The whole piece was communicated *only* in terms of music and dance, not in this instance narrative.

A pattern of day-long working sessions each week emerged. Other children would work in the usual way but the composer group worked with the outside composer. Each week the morning would be spent composing melodies and moods for unpitched and pitched percussion. Tunes, themes and melodies were produced for the relevant section. The 'bones' of each section were completed in three days over three weeks. By the end of each morning a 'score' was produced. A section would look like this.

In the afternoon the composers would teach what they had composed to the group of players. The players would spend some time practising the material while the composers began to compose parts for their own instruments (violin, recorder and piano).

It was interesting to see the discipline with which the composers drilled the players. Approximations were certainly not good enough. The 'composers' would hand over the score and one member of the composing group would explain the piece and what was intended to the players and then drill or rehearse them until the piece was perfect. At the end of each day everyone would listen to what had been achieved but this 'showing of work' was of most benefit to the group of dancers who would take the ideas and develop them in movement.

A small group of 'choreographers' worked on the dance ideas at first and were later joined by additional performers. The music, although taped, was capable of change and if, as often happened, the dancers requested changes, they would ask the composers to adjust their work. Perhaps a silence would be required, an aural cue (e.g. a bell was incorporated) or a particular rhythm. The music had to reflect the different dance styles that appeared in the piece: some elementary ballet, some tap and some contemporary dance. Tap was identified with one character who had particular musical themes and rhythms. There were crowd scenes and a large fight scene. The range of ability was used positively. Three 'guitarists' knew only three chords and, using them in sequence, they were able to compose a haunting, hounding section. Two older and more skilled dancers were given a solo and duet so that they, too, felt that they were being stretched.

Eventually a recording was made of the whole piece both on audio tape and video tape. It was important to have a sound recording as the video necessarily focussed on the dancing and the music deserved to be given a good quality audio recording. These were seen and heard by the students after the final performance and gave the piece a sense of value. Also photographs of work in progress were taken and dancers were able to study these and discuss their technique critically. Photographs featured in an exhibition at the school, which helped to focus the attention of outsiders on the process work rather than just the public outcome. The project required rehearsal, concentration and commitment and the whole was very professional.

Looking at performance in more detail

Usually a performer comes to a work with a certain amount of expertise in terms of *technique*. Broadly speaking technique concerns skills, not so much natural talent but learned expertise. It is technique that enables a singer to sing performance after performance or an actor to work in a particular style. Technique, natural talent and experience combine in professionals to produce excellence in a performer. Even amateurs need technique and in schools there's no point in relying only on natural talent. Teachers are in schools to teach, to nurture and extend children's experiences and abilities. Sometimes children are put into school plays either because they seem to have natural talent or because they can read a script well. In one infant school the children worked so well on establishing the characters that parents watching assumed that the actors had been typecast.

Skill and technique usually come after the initial enthusiasm but can be acquired systemically afterwards. If the learning is structured, every project or performance will require new skill acquisition. After every project the child performer should feel that if he or she were to start again they would be starting with more skill, knowledge or understanding. There's nothing wrong in having 'skills sessions' when useful techniques can be practised or learned. There's a fine line to tread between skills and creative work:

- too little emphasis on skills can mean that children are frustrated by their inability to achieve what they would like to do;
- too much emphasis on skills can seem tedious and without point.

On the whole teachers can spot when children are going to need extra skills work (this will be developed in Chapter 5 *How the performing arts fit into the primary curriculum*).

Skills in drama

A *regular* prog.amme of improvisation would benefit any performing arts work. Books giving such programmes are available and these

Figure 3   *Exercises designed to create trust within a group can be developed over a long period of time so that pupils learn to work together rather than competitively.*

tend to advocate an ongoing course of work which builds up over weeks, months or even years. One useful aspect of such work is that it draws on real life: observation of others, thinking about how people are and how they react, reliving situations.

Teachers will be aware of 'mirror' exercises. Children sometimes see such work as 'catching out' their partners. They learn, after practice, that this type of work helps children to collaborate and work together. When children in pairs try to mirror each other they will find that the skill is in working together in order to exclude the on-looker and not to try to outdo their partner. With practice children will become very skilled in this type of exercise. They can then use the 'mirror' as a prop by acting into it. 'You are looking into the mirror when you hear some bad/sad/good news'. This can be extended to a larger group where all are imitating each other and the outsider has to determine who is initiating the movement. As a group of actors doing this exercise the whole team learns to rely on each other. They can become less competitive in terms of their own roles. They can begin to learn that everyone involved in a creative arts project is interdependent.

Such exercises and more are listed in books on teaching drama. Regular practice helps to perfect them. All such programmes emphasise techniques and independence in the actors. Also some exercises address certain problems such as stilted delivery of words, lack of eye-contact with other actors, use of the body on stage. They usually provide the actor with an ability to understand a character on stage. Acting should not be the ability to learn lines, it should be about understanding how a character thinks, why he acts as he does, what is it like to be in someone else's shoes. If children feel happy with a character they will interpret her well for an audience. Short techniques sessions of about 10 or 15 minutes before a rehearsal can help enormously.

There are many styles of acting: acting in a soap opera in front of a camera is very different from acting in a Shakespearean play. Within the professional theatre actors often specialise in a particular aspect of acting. Children in primary schools will not be able to learn different acting styles but they will be able to grasp how to become a character, especially if they can identify with the character (for this reason it is better for children not to have to act as adult characters).

Acting: some guidelines

1 Children need to want to be actors. A stage is a very vulnerable place.
2 Find ways of auditioning or choosing children which relates directly to what they will do on stage and bears no relationship to their reading ability. A child reading a script will not necessarily understand how it should be read or where the actor should stand. This is the director's job. Children should be encouraged to think about situations that they might be put in on stage, can they relate to a character, sub-text of the character and adapt well on stage? In primary schools children are often chosen for actors because they are good academically. In secondary schools drama is sometimes considered suitable for the less academic. Academic ability is not really a consideration in this context.

3   Generally speaking it is best to ask children to represent other children on stage. It is virtually impossible for the average primary school child to understand how an adult thinks. This is the problem about asking children to act in roles which are outside the range of their own experience. At best the rendition will be 'cute' because the child is playing a role that was written for an adult. Although it is enchanting to see children looking amusing or quaint, it is also patronising. The arts work for children at their own level and age. It is unfair to put children in a situation where an adult audience will say 'It's good considering that they're children'. There is a range of writing with mostly child characters. Children will play child characters best (better than an adult) because they will understand how they think.

4   It is crucial that every member of the cast sees every role in a play as important. There is no room for the 'star' in educational drama. Every role, even the 'one-liner' is important for what each character is doing on stage even when he or she is not saying a 'line'. He or she needs to respond to others and remain in character on stage. It's very difficult to be mute on stage and easy to upstage another character.

A team of actors needs to get to know their characters using background information in the text.

- What does my character say?
- What does my character think?
- What do other characters say about my character?
- What do other characters say to my character?
- What does my character think about other characters?

There will be no right or wrong answers to these questions and a good deal of discussion and language skills developed when the actors compare notes.

Performing music

When performing a piece of music the main skill required is working with others. Many children are competent solo players and singers but when placed in an orchestra become lost. It is important to establish that rehearsal provides the opportunity for focus on interpretation ('let's try this louder/softer/faster/with more menace'), so that it becomes clear that the performers are interacting with the score and with one another to produce something as a group. Individual parts should be practised elsewhere. This is true of both a major presentation and an accompaniment for a hymn or song in assembly. Children will get used to the idea of group playing. Many song books now have simple arrangements for several players: tambourine, chime bars, recorders. The percussion parts, even if modest, are very important as the children learn how to play in a group, wait for their entry, play together and depend on one another.

When working on a score created by children it is important to have a conductor and quite important that the composers are around, so that if there is a problem of interpretation or technical difficulty they can be consulted. Professional performers often write for specific singers or players and pupils can do this too. Also if a player or singer says that he cannot manage a particular part, changes can be made.

Occasionally it is useful to include more skilled players, perhaps even a parent or a professional player. In the project described at the beginning of this chapter, professional string players joined the performance and carried the music to heights and depths which would not have been possible with the children alone. Watching the professionals rehearse in the body of the pupil orchestra encouraged the whole group in a professionalism that enhanced the performance. It is well worth finding out about musical ability in the locality. Older pupils who have left the school might be willing to come back to play. Parents, local amateurs and professionals might like to build up a casual relationship with schools in the area.

Stage direction

The teacher usually takes the role of director in any stage production although some teachers give this role to children. The director works with the actors and performers and can be assisted by a stage manager. It's important to differentiate between the roles of the director, performer and stage manager.

Here's an extract from a script written by top juniors:

Scene 3: The computer room

(Mavis and Bella enter very quietly. Mavis drops a coca-cola tin she has been drinking from)

MAVIS **Oooh, I've dropped my coke tin.**
BELLA **Where? (she falls over it) Oh there, thanks for telling me. (Mavis laughs. We hear the 'gang song' being sung off stage getting nearer)**

MAVIS **Oh no. Help! Someone's coming! It might be a teacher and they'll catch us having a look at the new computer. We'd better hide.**

BELLA **Where shall we hide?**

MAVIS **Here behind the screen. Quick.**

(In her hurry Bella trips over a waste paper basket)

The *actors* playing Mavis and Bella will:

- work out a background for their characters and know how they would expect them to react in this situation
- know why they were coming into the computer room at this time and where they have come from
- know how well their characters know the computer room (Do they know about the screen, for example, as this will determine how long it will take them to think of somewhere to hide)
- know the relationship between the two characters and the gang outside

The *director* will give them 'moves' or 'blocking'. She will know where they will enter and the position of the computer and screen. She will also decide when they move towards the computer and screen.

The *stage manager* will note these 'moves' in his script and if necessary rehearse the actors from time to time.

The teacher working as a director can allow plenty of discussion and negotiation over these points. Much work can be done sitting in a classroom discussing motivation, how things are said and why. This can be done with singers too. The quality of the singer's work is improved immensely by understanding of what is being sung and why.

Dance

Unfortunately because dance seems to communicate so directly, it is often assumed that it is an artform particularly suited to younger pupils and can, therefore, seem to them to be something that one grows out of. This is where the importance of a whole school policy comes in. The hidden curriculum can be examined in case there are subtle suggestions that dance is for infants.

- Do older students present their dance work to younger children?
- Are both boys and girls encouraged to dance?

- Do boys and girls have different perceptions about their ability to dance?
- Are pupils encouraged to create their own dance pieces?
- Are pupils encouraged to choreograph small pieces, perhaps within a larger drama production?

The peculiar status of dance within PE and 'across the curriculum' in the National Curriculum guidelines implies that teachers need to be particularly vigilant in order to give dance the status it deserves in school. Individual schools will have to establish their own aims for dance and ensure that, if taught within PE, it is systematically taught throughout the school and that, in addition to its position within PE it is allied to teaching in music and drama so that the 'humanity' of dance is stressed alongside the 'physicality'.

In a school production or showing of drama work, abstract scenes and places where emotional decisions have to be made provide opportunities for small choreographed sections. In a school project where a drama was evolved about life in a prison two choreographed sections depicting the prisoners' routine life and a riot proved central focus points for the musical drama and created a sense of the 'spirit' of the prison in a way that acting did not. Make-up and costume in sharp contrast to those of the actor prisoners emphasised this.

If funds and facilities (a good quality wooden sprung floor or linoleum is ideal) are available, it is valuable to invite professional dancers in to present a programme alongside children. A school group might work on a theme e.g. a folk tale, and could be assigned a specific section to work on from their own starting point. Perhaps original choreography could be used, or a multi-arts approach using story telling or visual images.

Organising a production

Where a particular performance is planned there's no real need to have access to the performing space that will be used for the final presentation, for every period of time devoted to the preparation of the performance.

A balance between creative work, acquiring specific skills of relevance to the project and the performance itself will ensure that a drawn-out rehearsal period will be less necessary than in the normal school production. Many teachers complain about school halls. They are often multi-purpose, being used as canteens, for PE and movement and for assemblies, and it is likely that most schools will not be able to provide unlimited access to such a multi-use space. Demands on the hall space need to be kept to a minimum. Most classes will be scheduled for large spaces at some time during the school week and such times, where possible, should be devoted to movement and dance where space is a necessity. A professional attitude to the design process (as outlined in Chapter 4 *Design skills and crafts*) helps children to be able to create/rehearse in other available spaces. A scale model can be used to talk through 'moves' and blocking. The discipline of working in a small space will delay moving to the staging too early, thus enhancing drama work because essential character analysis and individual characterisation can be done fully first. Also by working in this way there is an excitement when the actors and other company members move to the space in which they will actually perform the piece, and a flexibility if there is an intention to play the piece at other venues or for other audiences. The actor learns to relate to the piece and the acting area or world created in that area and not the physical space in which the piece will be performed. They should not be anchored by particular doors or windows in the school hall but by what is on their stage.

Rehearsing

A lot of work in preparing for a performance takes place in personal preparation and discussion. The longer the actual blocking is left, the easier it will be. It is unlikely, even in a school hall, that the pupils will have a vast acting area at their disposal and it is probable that the 'stage' area will not be bigger than the average school classroom. It is possible, therefore, to use the classroom for rehearsals. The (child) stage manager can mark out the performing space with tape or chalk. This will show exits, entrances, fixed scenery and other furniture, and will be capable of variation from scene to scene. This will also be of use when running the show later, as the stage manager will have plans for each scene and a properties chart which will show where each prop is at different points during the performance.

It is rare in most repertory companies for actors to have unlimited access to the space on which they will actually perform the play and even more unlikely in a major opera house or dance theatre. It is common professional practice, therefore, for rehearsals to begin in small studios with marked floors, to progress into larger rehearsal rooms with token or stock scenery and then to move on stage for the final run of rehearsals. In an opera house stage time is so precious

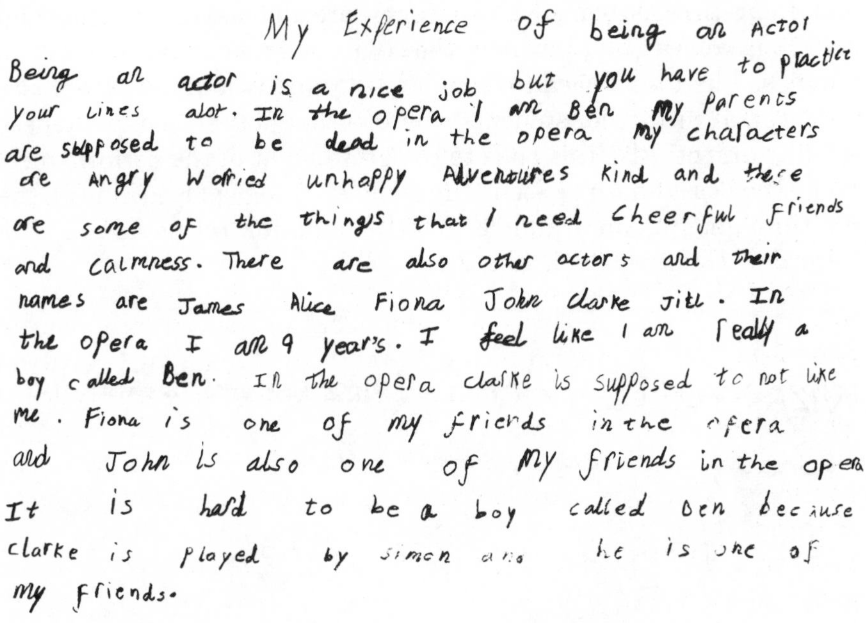

My Experience of being an Actor

Being an actor is a nice job but you have to practice your lines alot. In the opera I am Ben my parents are supposed to be dead in the opera my characters are Angry Worried unhappy Adventures kind and there are some of the things that I need cheerful friends and calmness. There are also other actors and their names are James Alice Fiona John clarke Jill. In the opera I am 9 year's. I feel like I am really a boy called Ben. In the opera clarke is supposed to not like me. Fiona is one of my friends in the opera and John is also one of my friends in the opera It is hard to be a boy called Ben because clarke is played by simon also he is one of my friends.

Figure 4   *This actor has done a good deal of work preparing for his performance and knows all about his character.*

that it is usual for each act of an opera to have only one rehearsal on stage with piano accompaniment and a further rehearsal per act with orchestra followed by the 'general' or dress rehearsal. Costumes are often only added for the orchestral rehearsals. This professional model is helpful to the teacher who has similar restrictions — availability of actors' time and accessibility to adequate rehearsal spaces.

It is theatrical practice for the stage manager to organise a call-sheet so that any rehearsal can take place in the most convenient fashion. This is especially helpful for major school productions where rehearsals take place out of lesson time and with pupils from across the school. The establishment of a noticeboard organised again by the child acting as stage manager or assistant stage manager can be the focus for the cast. The teacher, with the stage manager, can decide what needs to be rehearsed and when and pass this information on to the stage manager who will draw up a call sheet. If the teacher/director enjoys the luxury of being able to call children out of lessons for school-time rehearsals the call-sheet can be further refined so that children miss as little of other lesson time as possible. This *adds* to the status of the task as the pupils know that their time is being valued. They are not asked to attend an hour-long rehearsal in which they will only be required for 10 minutes. There's no need for pupils to sit quietly and listen to hours of rehearsal with other students where nothing other than politeness is being taught! Also this adds to the excitement of the performance; even the cast hasn't seen the whole thing played until the run-through. So, for example, a call-board for rehearsals of *The Wizard of Oz* might look like this.

WIZARD OF OZ Act I (Miss Roberts — School Hall)
Monday 6th Feb   2.00 – 3.30

2.00   Henry, Darryl, Jane, LeRoy

2.15   Above, plus Casdine, Simon, Akbar

2.30   Above, plus Sita

3.00   Full cast

Musicians, of course, could be called at different times by another teacher, as could dancers, singers or any other group of players. The skill is to organise everything so that it can be managed in small chunks and pieced together only at the very end.

Overall shape enables exciting things to happen. What may seem chaotic to the participants at first will come together in the end and make sense. Everyone will be able to see the direction in which they have been heading and will see real results at the end of each day, month, term or year. The outcome is progress and not frustration! This is why it is essential in any performing arts project to balance project and process and why end result *is* important. Both adults and children are encouraged by progress and success.

Whole projects involving creating and performing can be structured in this way and can integrate different age-groups. Imagine, for example, a project organised jointly for second and fourth year juniors. The aim of the project for the fourth years is to work on creating a piece of music theatre. The second year group is to be integrated into the 'performance' aspect. A typical schedule or structure could look like this:

Weeks 1 - 4

Throughout the project the 'composers' work in small groups.

One morning per week (fourth years): ideas for elementary compositional work building up technical skills, putting together an 'ideas bank' of tunes and 'mood music'.

Week 5

One morning:

- creating musical ideas for a choreographic piece to be played by fourth and second years and danced by second years.
- deciding on a theme for the dance, first ideas for percussion instruments.

One afternoon:

- presentation of 'work in progress' to the second year group
- explanation of work on the project to date, the theme, the musical ideas
- fourth year groups teach second year groups work to date and continue to compose for second years and for themselves.

Week 6

Mornings:

- fourth year groups continue to compose

Afternoons:

- showings of work
- fourth years present compositional ideas
- second years present choreographic ideas until the piece is complete.

If required other students work on set, costume and lighting design, stage management and find an audience for the final showing.

Week 7

Bringing together of all the ideas into one piece.

Rehearsals: stage manager organises space (who will go where?) with music and dance teachers.

Run-through and performances.

Working with different age-groups helps to differentiate between the creative work and interpretation. It also offers older pupils the possibility of focusing their work more clearly. In one school, a class of fourth year juniors made up song books for infants to perform. This meant that the first task was to visit the infant classroom to find out about the interests and skills of the infants. Also the older children went to the school library and borrowed books aimed at 6 and 7 year olds. Each child prepared a book for his or her newly composed song and illustrated it. The books were taken to the infant class to share with the younger children. Any comments and criticisms were taken back after the first showing and incorporated into the final version. The juniors recorded the comments of the infants and when the books were incorporated into the infant book corner the juniors visited the classroom to interview the infants about what they had read.

Sharing ideas

It can be helpful to have sessions when the children can explore ideas, outside the context of a project. They can be divided into groups and given a theme or word (storm/calm or happy/sad). Each group can work on illustrating the theme, either all in the same form (all through music) or with different forms (dance/music/drama/mime). When the groups have worked together for some time, they can show each other their work and try to guess what the given words were. This is specially helpful if it encourages discussion as to why some ideas worked for the audience and why others did not. The pupils can say why certain instruments, steps and words were used and those observing can say how effective the ideas were. With young children it's helpful to remember that most are not in possession of cliché representations or commonly known short cuts such as mime. This is liberating as it avoids cliché ideas. An original idea for representing say, a storm in movement and music is far more interesting than a predictable response.

After a 'showing of work' it can be helpful to discuss the outcome with the pupils and to build up a diagnostic approach with them. Do they need new skills? These skills can be introduced on an ongoing basis. The ostensible aim is merely to try out some ideas in the light of work recently done or new work yet to be started. There is no sense of urgency and material can be generated without fear of a deadline. It doesn't matter if there is only a small amount of material to show at the end. The group can try new techniques, new instruments, new media. Here are some ideas for music, drama, dance and design with the theme of 'space':

- A project in *music* might examine the 'spaces' or 'intervals' between notes on tuned percussion (keyboard) instruments. Groups could be allocated a set of notes according to the spaces between them. One exercise might be to take sets of three or four notes to try out tunes or patterns with them. Another exercise might use four notes that are very close together. Using the pattern method of evolving a piece described in Chapter 2 generates new ideas.
- In *drama*, improvisation techniques can be used to explore shapes in the air. Mime work can start with individuals showing use of a very small or a very large shape. Over a period of time this can develop to work in pairs, passing and catching, lifting and moving, using the task to take on all the peculiarities of the object (moving something heavy, dangerous, full of liquid). Gradually this type of scene can be taken on to a group exercise as a game or situation but with absolute concentration, so that every member of the group is aware and responds to the group situation. This sort of improvisation exercise, with dialogue added, can form the core of a scene, play or musical piece.
- *Dance* might develop from the mime, with movement and line added to the passing and catching work so that a simple piece could be choreographed starting with one or two dancers and gradually taking in a much bigger group. The pupils should work at developing a section with a beginning, middle and an end and, if building up numbers should prove sucessful, the exact moments for adding additional people.

When working on skills development the teacher can be nearby to suggest new ideas to groups and individuals. If, for example, a group of composers seems to be stuck with their own composition work, listening to a piece of music on a small tape-recorder with headphones might inspire them. Or if they were working on a simple tune, a tape of a piece of music with variations might suggest ways of making one 'tune' seem different. If the music is very conventional it might be interesting to play some different 'textures' or rhythms: natural sounds, African music, something with Hispanic rhythms or oriental themes. It is challenging to listen to music when it has a point of contact with the work in hand, so if a group is working on a musical piece about a storm it would be helpful to play Benjamin Britten's *Four sea interludes* from *Peter Grimes* or, if working on the theme of seasons the pupils might watch a video of the 'fairies of the four seasons' from Ashton's ballet, *Cinderella*. Many teachers keep records of such resource material, which can include:

- pictures and photographs
- music by professional composers
- videos of professional productions
- other stimuli including newspaper cuttings, reproductions of paintings, historical material.

4 Design skills and crafts

The Royal Opera in London and the Metropolitan Opera Guild in New York organise a project that encourages teachers to form a theatre company with young children. The project was devised by JoAnn Forman and Bruce Taylor of the Metropolitan Opera Guild. The scheme is very popular for obvious reasons: so much of what it encourages, exemplifies good primary school practice. Children can solve real problems they learn through doing, and they gain an insight into professional theatre and how it works. This chapter will examine how the roles in a professional theatre can be relevant to children in primary schools.

'Inside feelings outside' — a project with six year olds

A group of six year old pupils from a country school in Essex wrote, with their teacher, a piece called 'Inside Feelings Outside'. The piece was a play with music involving eight or nine children as actors, child musicians and the rest of the class of thirty working on all aspects of theatre organisation: stage management, prompting, lighting and public relations.

The piece was written in three scenes and concerned classroom bullying. The central character was a boy with whom no one wanted to play and who, therefore, found many aspects of school life, like going out to play, unpleasant. The first and final scene took place in the playground and the central scene in a classroom.

Stage design

A small group of children were chosen to be stage designers. Stage design offers three challenges and because the skills required are different from the skills fine art demands, the children set designers were not chosen for their ability to draw. Some key areas of set design are:

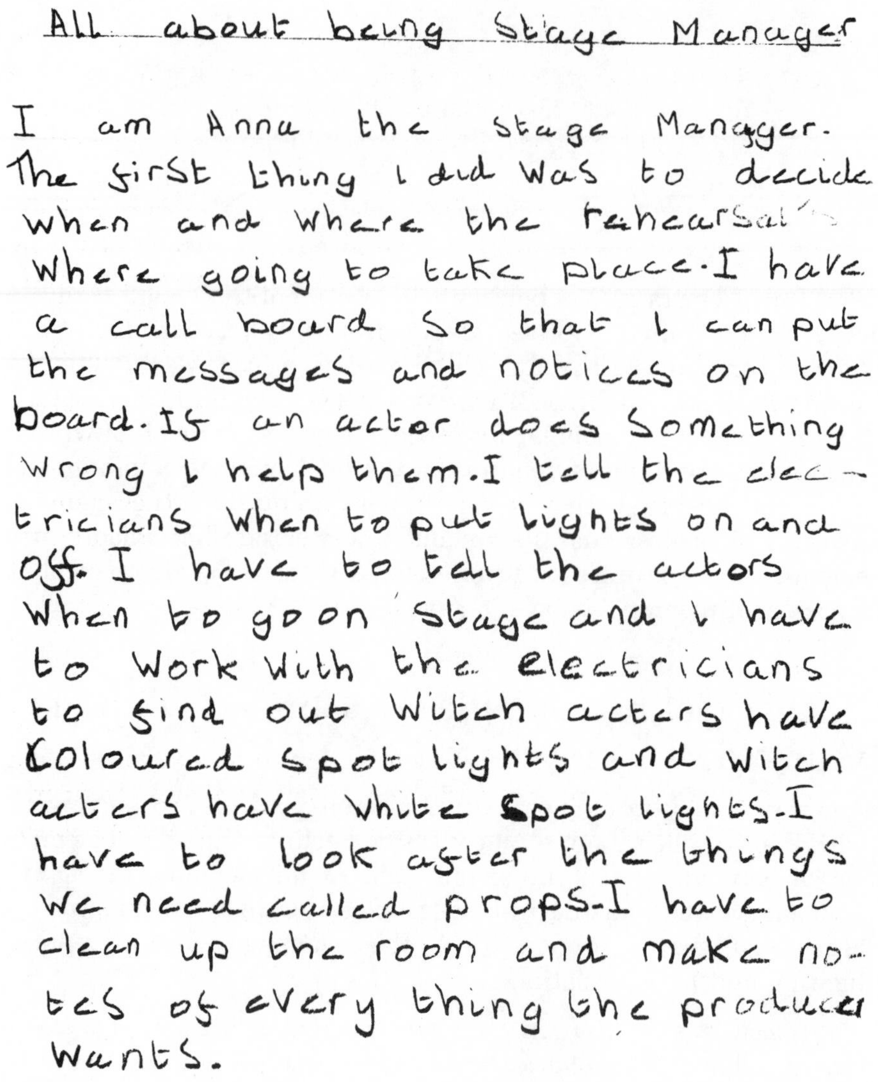

All about being Stage Manager

I am Anna the stage Manager. The first thing I did Was to decide when and where the rehearsal's Where going to take place. I have a call board So that I can put the messages and notices on the board. If an actor does Something Wrong I help them. I tell the electricians When to put lights on and off. I have to tell the actors When to go on stage and I have to Work With the electricians to find out Witch actors have Coloured spot lights and witch actors have White Spot lights. I have to look after the things We need called props. I have to clean up the room and make notes of every thing the producer Wants.

Figure 5   *Children are able to cope with what seem to be complicated professional roles, and can learn from doing them and taking responsibility.*

1 Problem solving

The task for this group of children was to solve the problem of how to stage the piece so that the story could move easily from outside to inside and back to outside and to create a space which would indicate where the scene was set and to enable the actors to move in and out of the scene. The entire piece lasted only about 35 to 40 minutes so it was very important that any scene changes were short.

If a piece has different scenes, the designer has to decide how to move the action from scene to scene. Also she will have to make allowances for what has to happen on the stage; the indication in the script might be for 'a shady wood' but the design concept will be influenced by whether there is a large choreographic section in the wood, or a quiet conversation. This is a problem solving role. The set designer is not necessarily a traditional 'fine artist'. She also has to make a visual statement about the piece. Sometimes the design can support the text and sometimes it can comment ironically on it. In any case it will be suggesting things to an audience in a visual way.

2 **Creating an atmosphere**
A second task was to create a mood for the play in a visual way. In the example above it was important that there could be a sense of isolation around the central character. Most importantly there was no need to recreate an exact school playground but rather to suggest to the audience that the scene was set in a particular place.

3 **Enhancing ideas**
The design needs to enhance the ideas of the writer, director and actors in a visual way. The designers were told their work would add to the work of the rest of the class. They could make their own statements about the script by what they chose to put on stage.

4 **Space**
The designers need to make the space available 'work' for the production. The infants above made decisions about basic things such as:

- Where will the audience sit? Calculations about numbers of chairs for the audience were necessary and the infants learned a great deal from working out plans of seating arrangements. They fixed a time when they could use the hall, try out seating plans and work out how many chairs could fit into the space. They marked out the seating area so that the actors knew the size of space left and made up charts with a box for each chair so that tickets could be made and sold.
- Where will the actors perform and change? Similarly they organised a special changing area in an adjacent classroom so that everything could be put out in advance of the perfor- mance and children could move freely between the hall and changing space.

- Where will the props be stored? (Some schools have a props table as in the professional theatre. See below.)
- Where will the piano be?
- Where will the actors' entrances and exits be?

Often children will not take an obvious route. If there is a traditional stage they might decide to place the stage area in the body of the hall, for example. Obviously there is no right answer to the question of set design. There are differing degrees of success in that some ideas may not work but in general there is usually a great deal of flexibility. The important factors are:

- Does it work visually?
- Does it work practically? For example a design probably doesn't 'work' if there are 3 minute scene changes between 2 minute scenes
- Have the designers used the limitations of the space to their own advantage? Interesting set designs have incorporated serving hatches, cupboard doors and staircases.

The first job for a set designer is to assess the space in which the piece will be presented. This is an ideal opportunity for mathematical work with real purpose. In order to create a design you need to find out about the space in which the play will be staged. So first the children made a sketch of the space where the piece would be presented. This was very rough at first but included doors, windows, other fixed items, electrical points and PE equipment.

Then the children came up with some basic drawings for the three scenes (the playground, the classroom and the playground again).

At this stage of first ideas the children did not distinguish between a drawing and a design and put people and backgrounds into their drawings, e.g. grass, sky and trees. This didn't matter as, at a later stage, when they come to realise the design they discarded this automatically. They created the image of a fence with litter bins for the playground. In its turn the fence proved a very flexible image representing inside and outside which was used in a direct way by the child working on the programme.

When Susan gave a short introductory speech to the parents explaining the production she picked up the image again.

In September we formed the Shooting Eagle Opera Company. We all auditioned for jobs. My job is Production Manager. I am in charge of carpenters, costume designers, set designers, public relations, make-up and electricians.

Figure 6 *Working as a professional. (Photo: Donald Southern)*

Figure 7 *Pupils learning to work in 3D. How does the forest look in the model box? Very different from a 2D drawing. (Photo: Donald Southern)*

We have had lots of visitors and help from the Royal Opera House. We would like to say thank you to all the people who came and helped and we give a special thank you for Dr. Hynd for helping to make the railings and Mr Perry for making the reflectors on the footlights.

'Inside Feelings Outside' is about how people's feelings can get hurt. We chose this title because during the opera people get hurt inside and outside. It is also set inside the classroom and outside in the playground.

We hope you like the opera.

Thus the children who thought up the image initially could see that they had produced an effective and worthwhile design which was, in turn, taken on by other pupils in the class for their own purposes. Everyone knew that the fence image was excellent. Not only did it set the scene but it also encapsulated the theme of the piece 'Inside Feelings Outside'. The local newspaper photographer even used the fence in a picture for his front page story!

Obviously the painting brought pleasure in itself but this had to be transformed into a stage set. The first obvious way was to make a model of the set so that the rest of the children involved could understand the idea. Model sets can be made with anything from lollypop sticks to plaster. The model enabled the actors to discuss their moves with the directors and other people in the cast. Where would everyone stand? How would they enter?

A first model, especially with infants, need not necessarily be to scale. A model of the fence and litter bins was made with lollypop sticks and wire. Models were made of each scene in order to show how the actors could move from scene to scene. The fence created some interesting mathematical discussion. There were fewer spaces than upright posts in the fence. Why was this? How much bigger would the 'real' posts have to be? They thought about how tall a child would be in relation to the model fence and worked out how long each post should be.

Next, a fairly accurate model of the space was made. Using squared paper and a manageable scale, the children were able to make up a ground plan of the performing space. They cut this out and put it in into a model box and then placed their model sets inside.

Older students were also able to make 3D representations, on small pieces of card, of moveable items such as the piano, stage blocks and sets of steps, which could then be moved around on the scale plan to give some idea about what space is available.

This became the *model box*. The model box was used with sketches and drawings to create a design concept in 3D.

This is very helpful because abstract ideas such as grandeur, chaos, intimacy can be developed directly in 3D. It can be useful to make a permanent model box of the school space. This can be kept somewhere handy so that the teacher can use it to talk through where children will stand for school assembly presentations, for example. In this way the pupils will get used to thinking of the model in terms of the actual space.

Passing on the design

The infant 'designers' had to pass their ideas on to those children who would make or assemble the scenery. The fence was made with cardboard tubes, the classroom scene required real desks, chairs and classroom furniture. The designers were on hand to ensure that the

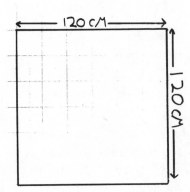

ICM = IOCM   A SCALE DRAWING OF THE SIDE STAGE

Figure 8   *Technical and accurate drawings are an essential part of set design.*

A SCALE DRAWING OF THE STAGE

SCALE
1cm=10cm

PILLAR B

PILLAR A

74 cm

74 cm

74 cm

74 cm

240 CM

5 M/110CM
AUDIENCE

Figure 9

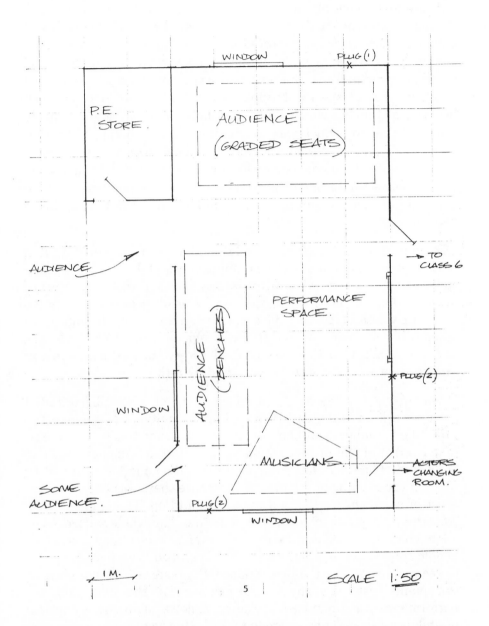

Figure 10 *A fairly detailed drawing on squared paper solves the immediate problem and helps mathematical understanding.*

actual scenery was in line with their ideas and were excited to see their ideas recreated in a larger format.

The need to pass on the design to others created a need to understand scale. Simple exercises in 'scaling up' proved to be great fun as well as obviously relevant. How could these young children indicate how much bigger than a drawing the real thing had to be? A simple drawing made by one of the children was doubled, and doubled again until the required size was found. It was relatively simple to arrive at a scale, for example three times as big. The drawings prepared for this exercise were not done for their own sake but with a specific purpose. The children could distinguish between a drawing which had taken hours of work and a quickly prepared drawing which was contributory to the solving of another problem. They could also see that they could try out ideas fairly quickly inside the model box or in drawings. They didn't have to go to the bother of bringing in heavy furniture or painting scenery. They could discuss different ideas and discard those that didn't appeal.

The importance of allocating roles and carrying them out in a professional way cannot be over-emphasised. Only if a job is done well can it achieve worthwhile results. Rather than the teacher being responsible for bringing in a few items of scenery and costume at a fairly late stage, to add authenticity, these top infants were responsible for every aspect of the design process. The result was that the children in the class created a very successful production and covered many aspects of curriculum work.

Carol Smith, the teacher, was an excellent enabler. She initiated project work and then stood back while the children carried out the task. She was always on hand to advise but happy to let the children take control of the project which became 'theirs'. At one point one child said 'The opera *has* to happen now. It's gone too far for it to die'. On the evening of the first performance there was a tremendous sense of ownership of the project by the children. They were sharing something very special with their parents. The whole village knew about the project. A local taxi driver when asked to take a group of people from a nearby station to the school said 'You must be going to see the opera!' For the performance, the teacher took her place at the piano just like any other member of the cast and the performance was organised by the child stage manager. Any group of children can organise a production in this way if a teacher is on hand to guide them through the stages listed above. It has to be remembered that *any* decision about the environment created on stage is a design decision, so not to light a set (or presentation) is also making a statement.

In another project the child designer worked closely with another pupil who was the Production Manager. As Production Manager Paul took responsibility for making sure the design group's ideas

DUNMOW
& BRAINTREE TIMES

Thursday, February 6, 1986

18p

aper for Dunmow, Barnston, Broxted, The Canfields, Chickney, Duton Hill, The Eastons, F
dsell, The Rodings, The Sampfords, Stebbing, Tilty and Thaxted. We're the really LOCAL I

OPERA pupils at Felsted crowd behind the school fence they have created for their production.

First opera

for Felsted

BUSILY preparing for their first opera production are pupils of Class Three at Felsted Primary School.

The opera, called Inside Feelings Outside, has been written by the children and 28 of them are taking part.

The performance is taking place tonight at 7pm

at the school and the opera is about how people's feelings can get hurt.

The idea for an opera came as a result of the Royal Opera House Education Unit's summer workshop for teachers.

Not only did the children — aged seven and eight — write the opera but they have also spent many hours making the scenery.

Figure 11   *Everyone knew that the project was worthwhile when it was front page news!*

were realised. He had a team of other children to help him to do this. This team included:

- carpenters who built the main prop, a large computer called Sid.
- scenic artists who managed to get hold of three enormous white sheets and to make them into backcloths which were each attached to fixed wall bars usually used for PE. The scenic artists took the designer's drawing and superimposed a grid which corresponded to a grid on the cloth. Each square was then copied

section by section onto the cloth. This is an excellent way of using measurement and scale drawing. Painted cloths need not necessarily mean a cloth at the back of a stage. They used the painted sheets tied to the tops of the wallbars. There were three painted sheets which were rolled up and fastened with cotton tape at the beginning. Children came on between the scenes and released the tapes revealing a new 'set' to the audience. At the beginning of the performance the sheets were rolled up and tied to the tops of the wall bars. At the beginning of each scene two stage managers came on and released the ribbons on one sheet. Each sheet represented a room or part of the school.

- costume makers who designed individual costumes and gathered them together for the actors.
- prop manager (prop is short for 'properties') who read the script and made a list of all props mentioned (e.g. packets of crisps, coca cola can) and anything from the costume designer's drawings. Having made the list he collected all the items and added to the chart the names of people from whom they had been borrowed. He also made up charts to show where the props should be at the beginning af Acts 1 and 11. He took responsibility for running the props table, making sure they were returned, getting them ready for the next show and returning them after the last performance.

There was a direct line of accountability, but within their job everyone took total responsibility. If something went wrong Paul would sort things out. In a professional company the *Production Manager* makes sure everything comes together on schedule and within a given budget. A team of carpenters or set painters will be assigned the problem of realising the set. In another project the children raised a small production budget by approaching local businesses. In this case Terry, the Production Manager, kept very detailed accounts of income and expenditure. Money was spent on buying make-up and some elementary lighting equipment.

The design concept can be in many styles. Imagine, for example, that you have a play that takes place in a supermarket. You do not have to have elaborate backdrops depicting a supermarket unless you want to. You can either have a realistic set or you can gather together some items that *suggest* a supermarket. In the second example students can have brainstorming sessions where they suggest items that remind them of a particular space or place.

Remember that set design is about problem solving and the main problem will be changing from place to place in the script. This is the challenge. Also the set design will be making a statement to the audience about *when* the piece takes place and *where*. Students should also consider such things as mood, atmosphere, use of colour which can suggest certain moods or suggest a change in time, for example from morning to evening.

When includes:

* period or date
* exact time

and will affect the setting, the costumes and props and details such as the hands on clocks, whether the actors are dressed for summer or winter, daytime or evening.

Where includes:

* country
* town
* building
* room

and will affect the scenery and props.

Sometimes a play takes place in several different places. In this case the set designer needs to work out a way of moving from place to place. A *story board* will help with problem solving. It can be used to show how the set changes for different scenes. Sometimes your play will be set in one place but there will be subtle changes (day/night can be shown with lighting). Books on making stage scenery and furniture are available and can be adapted for classroom use. Making accurate drawings, gathering furniture together within a design concept, or painting a backcloth from a drawing can all be the total responsibility of the students.

Simple ideas are often the most effective. In one school production the only constructed piece of scenery was a park bench which was made by the carpenters who then added graffiti to make it look more realistic. The piece was performed in the body of the floor ('in the round') and the park bench was on rostra (well-lit). This created, exactly, the setting required by the design team.

Costume Design

Ideally the costume designer should work closely with the set designer. Costume is a development of character in most pieces of drama. Alternatively it can make a design statement of its own. Children can probably learn most from the type of costume design

Figure 12   *Two ways of solving the same problem, either paint a backdrop or use items to suggest the setting.*

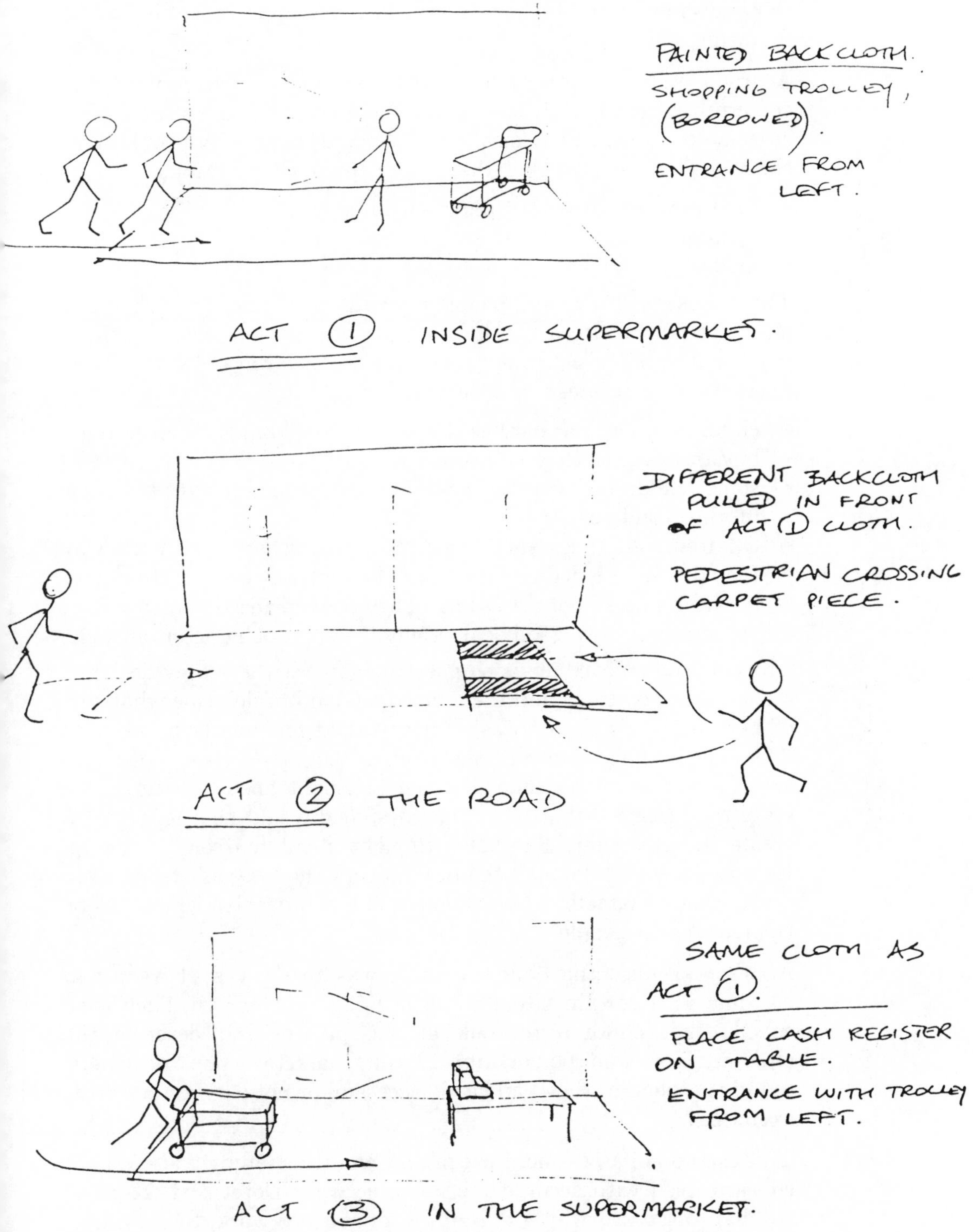

PAINTED BACKCLOTH.

SHOPPING TROLLEY,
(BORROWED).

ENTRANCE FROM
LEFT.

ACT ① INSIDE SUPERMARKET.

DIFFERENT BACKCLOTH
PULLED IN FRONT
OF ACT ① CLOTH.

PEDESTRIAN CROSSING
CARPET PIECE.

ACT ② THE ROAD

SAME CLOTH AS
ACT ①.

PLACE CASH REGISTER
ON TABLE.
ENTRANCE WITH TROLLEY
FROM LEFT.

ACT ③ IN THE SUPERMARKET.

Figure 13 *A storyboard is like a cartoon strip. It shows the action and makes the pupil think about how the scenery changes from scene to scene.*

that develops from the character and can approach this in the following way.

A group of top juniors wrote a play, set in wartime Britain and corcerning a group of evacuees. Two children were given the role of costume designers. First of all they thought about why people wear clothes. They decided that there were three main reasons:

- to stay warm in winter and cool in summer
- fashion
- modesty.

They began to study what people wore in school and why. They had a lot of fun collecting information. The reasons people chose particular items of clothing to wear were not always obvious. They made a list of interesting observations:

- children often wear clothes that are too big because their parents buy things that they will grow into
- some children have to wear things handed down by their brothers and sisters
- children sometimes show aspects of their character in the way they dress. This led to a survey. The children went on to devise questionnaires about dressing. They soon realised that items of clothing can say a good deal about a person or character on stage.

The children enjoyed devising guessing games, where they designed a character's costume and then asked a friend to describe what sort of person the character was. They worked out questions such as 'Does the character live in the town or country?' 'Does s/he like sport?' When the costume designers thought about costumes for stage they realised that what they designed would help an actor to create the character. They also thought about hair and make-up. Because they had done all the groundwork they weren't tempted to create cliché characters. For them the characters on stage were to be treated as real people.

Another exercise the children tried, was to draw a character in costume in a certain situation (e.g. going to a party). They then asked other children to look at the picture and describe the circumstances and personality of the character. The 'designers' found out whether they had been successful or not as a result of this exercise.

This method of assessment is fun and non-threatening and does not concern itself with accuracy as much as with 'Does it work?'. The children discussed why a design did or did not work. Some things were controversial. Sometimes the designer was trying to say something which was confused when 'read'. One boy costumed a character in a hand-me-down coat to show 'a large family' which was 'read' by a friend as meaning 'poor'. In such a case the designer obviously needed to think again, bearing in mind that the designer has every right to stand by her design. The audience might need training to read the designer's signs!

Even if the characters are less concrete than everyday people (martians, for example) there should still be a design concept and a sense of character in each costume design.

In the case of designs for the evacuees the designers had to go to the school library and do some historical research. They found out what children would have worn during the war years. They also found out more general information about the period, including details such as the use of gas masks. They then came up with designs that both reflected the historical period and demonstrated characteristics of the children in the play.

Make-up and props

In a project with a group of eight and nine year olds the teacher decided to ask a group of children to think about make up design. The task was to design the make-up for a ten year old boy who has just come in from football, having scored the winning goal on a frosty December day. Some children really understood the task and the outcome provided a focus for discussion about make-up design.

In this instance it was important for the children to think about the task and to look at people's faces noting the differences made by age (e.g. wrinkles, beards), physical differences (e.g. freckles, shape of face) and mood (e.g. grief, good news). Some children found they could think imaginatively about make-up. Having worked on a make-up design for a child character they then tried to adapt what they had done to show how the character's face would change after a football match, or swimming. They could also add make-up to create subtle differences such as change of mood.

The practical aspect of the make-up artist's job is gathering the necessary 'tools of the trade' together and practising applying the make-up. In this instance the teacher asked the make-up artists to make up the entire cast. This helped to develop trust between the actors and the make-up artists. It also gave status to the task, as the actors became aware of the complexity of make-up design and its importance to the whole 'design' concept.

The children were given a small budget and asked to make a list of

MAKE-UP

IN-SCHOOL PROJECT

(Follow-Up to Session #1)

PRODUCTION/TECHNICAL SHEET

Name: Elena Carramanta

Class: 5/4

Name at least four different reasons make-up is used:

1. You can use make up to cover up bruises

2. To make your face noticed, to stand out.

3. To disguise yourself.

4. To create a character on stage for a play or theatrical reson

Name at least four ways in which you can use make-up for theatrical purposes.

1. To show scares, bumps, bruises etc	2. To make your face show up when lights are shined on you
3. To show which colour face your ment to have (white, brown, light brown etc)	4. To show what character you are playing

For each one of the ways you use make-up for theatrical purpose, list what you would need to do it:

1.	2.	3.	4.
Dark blusher Dark eyeshadow (special make up putty for bumps) eyeliner pen (or a dark pencil)	Bright eyeshadow, Bright lipstick, Blusher, eyeliner, mascara	Coloured face cover cream, Blusher, Mascara, Black or brown eye liner penci (to paint on lines and rinkles)	eg (clown) White cover paint Bright red or pink lipstick to make lips bigger, red lipst for cheeks (circles) Black eyeliner to make eyebrows higher and to show lines on the face

P.T.O

Figure 14 *Pupils need to think imaginatively about what can be achieved with make-up.*

Figure 15   *Can the pupil be encouraged to use make up to show emotion?*

what materials they thought they needed. They thought of a mirror, spotlight, paper towels, sponges, hair grips, tissues, q-tips, old-towels and cold cream. Some of these things were easily obtained or borrowed. The children had to think about hygiene and arrange for old towels to be washed.

They then started to think about the make-up itself. They sent for catalogues from a well known make-up shop and found the prices high. This meant that the children needed to consider what was essential and what could be adapted. They realised that they could buy large sticks of foundation and cut them into two rather than buying individual sets of items for several people to use. The basics included pancake foundation, shader, rouge, highlighter, eyebrow pencil, lipstick and powder.

A make-up chart was developed for each character. In some cases when characters were wearing a normal 'straight' make-up, a chart for this covered all but the unusual characters (old people, fantastic creatures or characters with special features e.g. scars, wrinkles).

The entire design team needs to assemble costumes, make-up and sets in a business-like way. In the case of costumes, the designers must know what needs to be made or borrowed, and organise this. If items are borrowed, a record must be kept of where they were obtained, along with an 'actor by actor' sheet listing all the items of clothing and props, plus the actor's measurement and name. This can be copied onto individual labels and attached to each costume

Figure 16   *Every aspect of the actors' costumes has to be there for a purpose.
Good costumes help the actor create the character.*

on a hanger so that the costume designer (or, if preferred, the *wardrobe manager*) can gather everything up after each performance and check items against the list. The label can also be used when the costume is dismantled and returned to the appropriate places. An infant class organised costumes in this way. They borrowed a costume rail from a local charity shop and arranged all the characters' costumes on hangers, attached labels with the name of the actor and character and a complete list of all the parts of the costumes. Then there was a list at the end of the rail of all the costumes stored there so that the children could mark all the costumes out and in, check them and make any repairs.

Props, too, are 'designed' in exactly the same way, so that any item appearing on stage both fits the design concept and the characters. If a character has to carry an umbrella, for example, any umbrella will not do. It has to be the type of umbrella that the particular character would use.

Props, of course, offer scope for making things, in plaster, papier-mâché and clay. Masks are very useful and can be made simply with plaster bandaging or papier-mâché. It's usually best to make masks that cover only the top half of the face as this gives the actor flexibility. It would be possible to develop a very impressive programme of craft work devoted to the creation of props that are actually needed!

An historical perspective

In order to understand that costume reflects character and that scenery reflects life, a child needs to relate these ideas to the present. During a project on 'Ourselves' some children asked' 'What makes my bedroom mine?' They decided that it was the objects chosen, the care (or lack of it) with which they were placed, the state of the decoration, the things left all over the floor. They thought about different circumstances of families they knew. They thought about representing a room of a family with a new baby and a toddler. They thought about how they could suggest this on stage. They thought of felt pen marks on the wall, building bricks under a chair, a play pen in the corner. The children considered other scenarios with older children in the family or grandparents' homes.

It was quite easy to consider the point that even if every child in a class were to wear the same uniform, they would still need to be costumed differently — Jamila's skirt is too short (Why? She can't afford a new one); James has no tie (Why? He's lost it again). Every classroom in the school is different and the difference depends on the children in the class, the teacher's attitude and the physical position of the space.

To deal with a historical period means going through *all* the above and *then* adding the historical perspective. This can be very valuable in history based topics. Ideally, older pupils tackling a historical project will have been through the processes above and will bring an understanding of character to the new subject. In costume terms there is no stereotypical 'Victorian' costume, any more than there is a stereotypical costume for the late 20th century. Also there's a need to take care, when matching up costumes from historical books on fashion, with characters on stage. Imagine what such a book might depict for, say, 1970 or 1980. Would everyone wear up-to-date fashions? In a family how would mother, daughter and grandmother interpret the fashions? Older people often 'stick' with a fashion from an earlier time in their lives. So people dress according to character within the fashions available to them and the resources at their disposal. Knowledge of the character (e.g. rich or poor? old or young?) is still vital, and research into the historical period will provide the starting point that comes automatically with contemporary dress. To point out the sense of non-stereotypical dress ask the child to imagine a ten year old girl wearing her grandmother's clothes, or a farmer going to work dressed as a doctor.

Drama, too, can suggest ways of understanding the relevance of history. By analysis of characters within an historical context a child can begin to empathise with the individuals involved in any one situation. This can occur by using drama as a vehicle for understanding, or by creating a piece of theatre about the period in question. An example of this was a project with primary school pupils in Cornwall centred on a local National Trust property at Lanhydrock House, Bodmin. Over the course of the project the children researched the history of their own area, going back to late Victorian times. Their researches took in daily life, industrial relations, diet, and national politics. Throughout the project they were able to learn appropriate dances, songs and verses for the period and to reconstruct local events, such as the closing of tin mines. They soon began to see the complexity of the issues involved and the different positions adopted by the poor and the mine owners. No issue is ever as simple as it appears in a child's history book and so by working through the characters the children could appreciate the complexity.

Lighting design

Much can be communicated through lighting and a group of children can be given the task of working through a play, dance or musical and putting in lighting cues.

A very simple example from a class of infants was the lighting design for a particular song, sung by the characters who made up in class, a piece about 'Feelings' mentioned earlier. The song, written and composed by the class was as follows:

> (KAREN)......**I'm glad it's playtime then I can run around,**
> (TEACHER)... **I'm glad it's playtime so I can have my tea,**
> (ALEX)..... **I wish it wasn't playtime 'cos they all bully me.**
> (LOUISE).... **I'm glad it's playtime I can play a game**
> (SUZANNE)....**I'm glad it's playtime I can eat my tuck,**
> (ALEX).....**I wish it wasn't playtime 'cos they all bully me.**

The stage was lit with footlights and general lighting for lines one and two but was dimmed for line 3 when Alex (the bullied one) sang, thus creating a change of mood which reflected a change to the minor key for Alex's sad line.

Such lighting plots can be devised for the very simple stage lighting found in most schools and can be planned even if local regulations insist on adults actually operating the switches. Pupils can also cue the lights to be put on and off at the appropriate moment during the performance, and can work out when it is appropriate to make lighting changes.

The design elements of theatre can apply directly to the school production and can enable the learning of many skills, for example, mathematics, science and craft. Also, it is possible for students working in this way over a number of years throughout the school, to build up considerable expertise in these areas and to compare their work with other productions or class work. In this way critical skills are developed.

Communication skills and the real world

In reply to the question "What is 'Public relations' about?" an eight year old replied "Public relations is about getting on with people. We asked business people to give us money for our play. If they did we sent them a free ticket. If they didn't they didn't get a free ticket".

Public Relations is a little more sophisticated than this would suggest, but the performance arts do bring opportunities for Arts Marketing and PR which relate directly to the real world and raise interesting issues about the role of a performance and the artists involved in it.

Pupils dealing with PR often look at such questions as :

- how will people hear about our play/dance/opera/musical?
- how will we know who is coming?
- how should we look after people who come?

The answers to such problems involve work in graphics, communication and skill with words. It is conceivable that even a simple school production (or indeed class presentation) could benefit from:

- a *poster* designed to attract attention and inform those reading it of time, place and event. A small group in a Northamptonshire school were so pleased with their poster design for their musical that they decided to take it to a local printer who offered to print it for them free of charge and to show them how it was done. Two children took a video camera along so that those children who couldn't go to see the printer at work could see it back at school. A lovely poster in three colours was produced using the children's own artwork.
- a *programme* designed by the students, providing information about the piece, the actors, the origin of the project and a breakdown of scenes. It also provides an opportunity to thank anyone who has helped with the project and even to sell advertising space. Here the printer suggested that the children might pick up the image in the poster for the programme cover, which they did to great effect.

Major school productions could also involve:

- *Tickets* for use by a child acting as a Box Office Manager. This provides opportunities for use of a wordprocessor or computer so that children can devise ways of printing large numbers of tickets and also working charts indicating which tickets have been sold and for which evenings. Students sometimes work out colour coding for different performances and different prices for other children, OAPs and even for different parts of the school hall. Children can also be involved in looking after and reserving seats for special guests.
- *Press and publicity*: children of all ages enjoy working with the press and can produce a press release and follow it up with a telephone call if the headteacher will allow it. There is a sense of

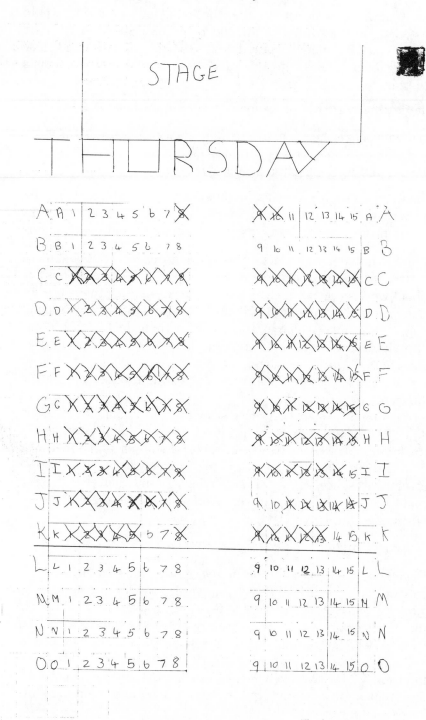

Figure 17 *The exercise of relating chairs to spaces and tickets to chairs helps pupils to think logically and develop organisational skills.*

Star Enterprises

BISHOPS TACHBROOK C.E. COMBINED SCHOOL

Kingsley Road, Bishops Tachbrook
Leamington Spa CV33 9RZ
Telephone 0926 26020

Dear
We are Howard and Dawn,the Press Officers of "Star Enterprise Company".As you can see in the enclosed press release we have written a play called "The Ancient Enigma".The duration of the play is approximately 40 minutes.The company is made up of children in the top two classes of the above school.We know the production will be a great success and we are hoping to perform it to different audiences other than in our village.We are writing to offer you the chance to let us perform at your school.As this is our first performance we would like the audience to be limited to those who might be interested in such a production.We are able to offer the last week of term as the dates we can show the play.These dates are 14 to 18 of July,1986.If you are interested in the offer please contact us by phone as soon as possible (the phone number is above) in order to make the arrangements of when we can perform.

Yours sincerely,
Howard Davis & Dawn Brown
(Press Officers)

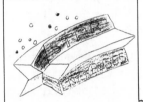

A NEW OPERA

The STAR ENTERPRISE COMPANY announce the launch of their first sparkling production.

Later this year the "Star Enterprise Company" will be performing an opera called the **Anciento Enigma**.So far in the production we have been designing the props and costumes, and have written the script. To record what we have done we are videoing it on a video camera.The Star Enterprise Company is made up of two classes of Bishop's Tachbrook Combined School.

The composers of the company are: Brendan Hole, Peter Simpson and Fiona Hayles. The writers are: Kevin Read, Dawn Brown, Lorraine Thomas, Sarah Woodfield, Tracey Elliot and Kim Gregory.The age group of the company is between 9 and 12 years.

We have been to places including **The Loft Theatre** in Leamington Spa to see what goes on behind the scenes. This is the first project the Star Enterprise Company have attempted and we hope it will prove to be a success. This\production is the result of **The Royal Opera House** education unit's summer workshops for teachers in association with **The Metropolitan Opera guide**, U.S.A. The Royal Opera House has sent us letters to explain what we should do in the coming weeks. We hope that more experts from the Royal Opera House will be able to visit us in the near future and help make this company a success.

Star Enterprises c/o Bishop's Tachbrook C.E. Combined School
Kingsley Road, Bishop's Tachbrook, Leamington Spa
Telephone Leamington 26020

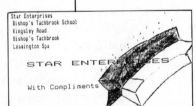

Star Enterprises
Bishop's Tachbrook School
Kingsley Road
Bishop's Tachbrook
Leamington Spa

STAR ENTERPRISES

With Compliments

Figure 18   *Public relations provided a reason for writing, editing and good presentation.*

the importance of a project if, for example, a company name for the group is established and there is a logo and company stationery. Children will soon realise that such a letter requires a contact name, address and telephone number and exciting, readable copy.

There can be opportunities for press and pupils to photograph a rehearsal for the local paper or for a display about the production. Liaison with the press can help children to understand how journalists work and can lead on to other 'hands on' projects such as editing a newspaper.

It would also be useful and interesting to make a video of the project from rehearsal to stage. A word of warning on the latter: ideally any video recording should be done properly, with storyboard and editing, not in an amateur way. In school it is important to convey these skills properly from the beginning, so that whatever is done in school never has to be undone and relearned in the proper fashion. Usually there is an expert in the LEA or in a nearby College of Further or Higher Education who would be willing to advise.

A group of primary school pupils worked on a film project which took a number of weeks. Rather than beginning with camera work, the team first prepared a narrative. Then they looked at their story in terms of a film: the setting could be indicated by a shot of the school sign; the passing of time could be shown by the burning of a candle on a birthday cake. The children prepared a story board which, rather like a cartoon story, showed exactly what the viewers would see at each moment. This could be used without editing facilities if the actors were well rehearsed and each shot had only one take but editing facilities obviously allow far more flexibility.

Photographs of the production can be reprinted for children to buy and to make an album for the school archives. Again this can be presented in a professional way with the production credits in the front and a cast list. Each photograph can be labelled with a short description of the scene and names of the actors. Also photographs of the project work that led up to a performance, such as set designs can be included. In later years children can look at photographs or video records of class and school performing arts projects, and learn from them.

Graphics and printing can be included in a theatre arts project and can be developed throughout school, thus encouraging a high standard of work in this area. Ideally pupils should work out a coherent scheme for public relations so that ideas for image, logo and stationery all reflect one another. This encourages group identity in the class and provides easy eye-catching material for

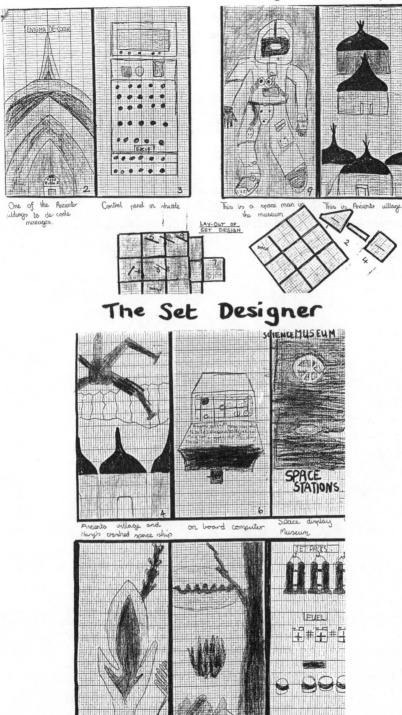

Figure 19 Set design provides opportunities for problem solving and imaginative art work.

onlookers. A company name continues this idea and often leads to design ideas. It also takes the performing arts project into a separate area of interest from normal classroom work and turns the project into something *really* special.

Notes

Phaidon, Oxford have published a series of 'Theatre manuals' (Series Editor David Mayer 1988) with the following titles:
Directing a play Micheal McCaffery
Lighting and sound Neil Fraser
Stage design and properties Michael Holt
Costume and make-up Michael Holt
Stage management and administration Pauline Menear and Terry Hawkins.

5 How the performing arts fit into the primary curriculum

Although guidelines for implementing the National Curriculum appear by subject area, it is quite clear that, in order to ensure that targets outlined by subject are met, they need to be integrated into a cross-curricular method of teaching and learning. The performing arts can, of course, be used, as vehicles for learning in other subject areas and can combine the demands of many subject areas. The performance arts are scattered across the guidelines with differing status. Dance, for example, exists within PE while music has an area of its own, with attainment targets. Drama takes its place within English and Language. It is important to recognise that *only* by integrating the arts can an ongoing arts programme be achieved. Within a week's workload it is impossible to ascribe the relevant percentages of time to each subject area. An arts programme can become a cohesive way of bringing together unrelated subject areas to the mutal benefit of both. It can reinforce both.

Teachers are sometimes anxious about reaching targets within subject areas when working in a cross-curricular fashion. However, the problem is not about legitimising cross-curricular work. The serious problem arises when one tries to approach the National Curriculum through subject areas alone. Learning cannot easily be compartmentalised by subject. Cross-curricular work enables the students to make connections, consolidate their learning and to think across subject barriers.

If we look specifically at the arts in terms of skills listed in the HMI *Curriculum Matters: The curriculum from 5 to 16* we can see that the performing arts fit happily into all the categories.

1 *Communication skills:* Drama and writing provide obvious vehicles for conversation and spoken language. Music, dance and art provide vehicles for non-verbal communication. Writing for communication purposes in publicity about arts projects is also important.

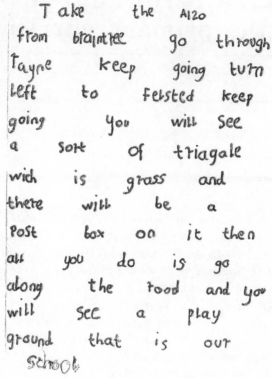

Take the A120 from brajntree go through tayne keep going turn left to Felsted keep going you will see a sort of triagale wich is grass and there will be a Post box on it then all you do is go along the road and you will see a play ground that is our School

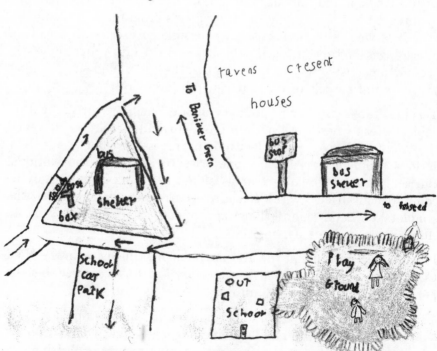

Figure 20 *When outsiders are invited to a school production they need clear instructions showing them how to get there!*

2 *Study skills and observation*: Good practice in writing and drama provides opportunities for editing, re-working and drafting. Work using historical source material is particularly effective in encouraging worthwhile and meaningful opportunities to develop study skills.

3 *Problem solving skills*: The arts offer opportunities for real problem solving. Every creative project or performance presents a number of problems needing imaginative solutions.

4 *Physical and practical skills*: Development of skills in movement, ability with musical instruments and techniques and practical ability in art and design are essential to any well-planned arts project.

5 *Creative and imaginative skills*: The arts are primarily about creativity and imagination, and are balanced by the practical skills mentioned above.

6 *Numerical skills*: Most people expect numerical skill to be unnecessary in the arts but, as Chapter 4 suggests, when the arts and arts projects are centred in the real world they provide a wealth of opportunities for science and maths work.

7 *Personal and social skills*: The performing arts can bring a sense of interdependence and personal development. Children learn to work together, to support one another's work and to empathise with others through drama and the arts.

Approaching topic work through the arts

In Chapter 1 a simple theme 'Characters' was discussed. Other themes for topics have been alluded to throughout this book:

• Feelings
• Families
• People around us.

Primary school teachers work in a variety of ways. Some choose particular projects for class work, others work with members of staff on a series of appropriate topic work over a number of years. Occasionally a headteacher will insist on emphasising a particular area of the curriculum in each term. A common breakdown is:

	Emphasis on:	Topics or Themes:
Term 1	Science Environmental studies	Insects Colour and light The sea
Term 2	History Humanities	Our village Buildings around us How we used to live
Term 3	Language Arts Religious Education	The theatre Stories from around the world

Other headteachers provide stimuli and allow the pupils, with careful guidance, to follow their interests and investigations while leading them on to exploit their enthusiasm in an area of learning to the full.

Whatever model of cross-curricular work the teacher or staff employs, the arts can provide a cornerstone. The performing arts are flexible, they involve the practical and the imaginative, the core subject areas and those on the edge.

Two possible approaches to using the arts for cross-curricular work are:

- approaching a topic or area of interest through the arts. Theatre in Education can work like this or approaching a history or environmental topic using dance, music and drama.
- using an arts topic to stimulate cross-curricular work. This type of work might include using a theatre visit or repertoire work as a basis for learning about a variety of subjects. Teachers often take a group to a performance of, for example, a ballet or play and use this to stimulate creative work drawing on themes and issues in the work. A ballet like *Swan Lake* can act as a springboard for topic work from studies of swans to composing music on the theme of good and evil.

Victorian Christmas 1893: a historical project

Over the course of one Autumn term a group of children worked on the theme of 'The Victorians' as a cross-curricular topic. Over the three month period they immersed themselves in things Victorian: finding out about the people, Britain in the late 19th century, interviewing grandparents and looking into record books and school documents. Over the course of a school term the children collected an impressive number of photographs, letters, account books and other interesting material which was gathered from parents and older local people. They processed the information, finding out first about their own village at the time and then looking at the county and country. They practised some of the crafts of the time, making Christmas cards and samplers. A Theatre-in-Education team visited the school and introduced a narrative element about the period. As the schools were in Cornwall, it centred on the tin mines. In the class, children were allocated roles, poor or wealthy children of parents who worked in or owned the mines. The children (aged between 7 and 11, vertically grouped) were then able to research their characters. They found out how much money such a family would have had, about schools, working conditions, even about the original Cornish pasties with savoury and sweet filling side by side in one pie. In music, local Cornish carols were introduced. A situation was then introduced. One of the wealthy mine-owners had decided to close the mine. The children, still in character, were able to respond to this. How would they survive? What repercussions would this decision have? This simulation exercise provided a focus for several hours of work involving discussion about the issues involved.

Another aspect of the project came in the form of an invitation by the staff of a local stately home, Lanhydrock House (owned by the National Trust), in Bodmin, to attend a Christmas party given for the children of tin miners. Earlier in the term the children had spent a day at the house and had used the visit as part of their project work. Some had taken photographs, others had taken sketch pads or taken notes. All read about Lanhydrock House and its history. The reconstruction of a Victorian Christmas required the children to learn appropriate dances for presentation at the party. They set to work learning what might have been danced, sung and acted. Along the way they found parlour songs, Victorian country dances and recitations. Also they researched Victorian clothing and each prepared a costume to wear on the day. Examples of work in handicraft were displayed at the 'party' and there was an exhibition of the children's work for those visiting the house. The period was thoroughly researched to a point where the children began to understand the implications of being a Victorian child. 'Would you have like to have been a Victorian?' received the reply 'Not a poor one!' On the day of the party the children arrived in Victorian costume with their Cornish pasties packed for lunch and were received by actors assuming the roles of lord and lady of the house.

'Other' Victorians able to sing and present ballet excerpts were on hand to entertain.

The arts element of the project provided an additional focus for the project and enhanced a straightforward topic by:

- giving the children a reason to find out about clothes of the period and making them think carefully about costume: what would a *poor, Cornish*, Victorian *child* have worn for a party at the home of local landowners? A context was provided for research.
- enabling the children to talk and work with people outside the school who could give them useful and interesting information. In this case the children talked to parents and grandparents about their work, the actors involved in the reconstruction, staff at Lanhydrock House and singers and dancers who visited the schools.
- enabling the children to discuss issues about the period in an informed way.
- providing a final event that summed up all that had been achieved throughout the term. By the time of the 'performance' a retrospective exhibition of the term's work had been presented. The children had designed and made costumes and they were able to participate in the reconstruction of the party and to present their singing and dancing. They were reminded of their earlier visit to the stately home and the final showing had the atmosphere of a party and a 'finale' to the project.

Working from historical documents

Another 'way-in' to an historical project would be to work from contemporary 'texts'. The *'Living Archive'* project produces a project book with examples of how school groups have used documentary material, interviews with local people and other local memorabilia as a starting point for putting together drama work, exhibitions, festivals and other projects. An example of such a project might take a photograph of a family group and use it as a basis for discussion and drama work. Evidence could be internal or external. What is the date of the photo, for example? How do we know that the date is correct? Features such as dress could give a fairly accurate indication. But by supplying students with some more accurate information about the picture it would be possible to get them to sympathise with the characters, their situation and lifestyle and to

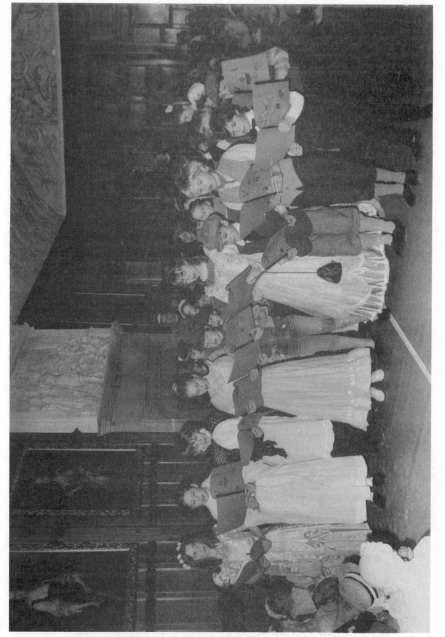

Figure 21 A 'historical' setting can provide interesting opportunities for understanding the circumstances of children in other times. Long skirts affect how you move!

get an insight into the historical period in question. This is where simulation work comes in. The children can 'really' become the characters and be placed in situations where they make relevant choices.

The date of this photo is 1917. The father's clothing (a military uniform) suggests (correctly) that the picture has been taken for the father to take back to the Front during the First World War. This should lead to a great deal of research into the period. For example, dates of the war, reasons for it, how it affected the lives of Britons and their families. Other material such as writing (poetry, for

Figure 22 *A photograph can generate discussion. Who are/were these people? What was their daily life like at the time of the picture?*

example) and music could be examined and visits to churchyards and a war memorial could be made.

The photographer's name and town are marked in the bottom left hand corner of the photo. In this case the photo was taken in Ely, Cambridgeshire. A teacher would, of course, tend to use a photo that related to the area near the school, as this would lead to humanities work relating to local history. It would not take much effort to work out the type of work that the soldier in the photo would have carried out in a fairly remote Fenland village in Northern Cambridgeshire in the early part of the 20th century.

Informed speculation about the names of the adults and children would be profitable (and could be compared with a study of current popular names as announced in the local or national papers) and could lead on to a study of social class. From here one could further speculate on lifestyle, income, diet, schooling and the prospects of the children in the picture.

When we discussed costume design earlier, a series of questions about character background were asked. Here one would ask them in reverse. By 'reading' the photos one could suggest something about the people there. Each character could be studied by a group of children. It would be possible to look out for subtleties.

• Winter or summer?
• Hairstyle and age.
• Footwear.
• Any evidence of teenage style? (Compare the dress and hair of the older girls and the mother with the two younger girls)

Having built up the characters in this way it is quite possible for the group to work 'in role'. They should now all know the names, ages, interests of their characters. A visit to a local cemetary could establish names very easily. They can improvise discussions between the characters, reactions to circumstances like father's leave, letters from the Front and times of hardship. Also it should be possible to examine independent evidence about the period, for example poems (for older children), postcards from the Front, contemporary newspaper stories, posters, a visit to a local or national museum with items of interest. Such items can be mocked up as 'props' for role-play.

Scene setting can look into what was current in 'the arts' at the time: songs, music, dance styles, entertainment and fun. This can be done at both a local level (these characters) and the wider level (important compositions of the time). Other contemporary material might help in set design. What did the house, town, countryside look like at this time? Music and songs can be created, based on stories from the time. Evidence from local people, archive copies of local papers, visits to old people's homes can provide evidence and information.

It would be a relatively simple thing (given all this background) to produce a simple 20 minute presentation about the lives of these people with appropriate music, dance and acting about a very simple event e.g. Armistice Day or the arrival of a particular piece of news or letter. Such a piece should be mindful of exact period setting and costume, and customs (how would women be treated, for example?) and could, reasonably, be peppered with appropriate readings of prose, poetry and fairly standard material (e.g. letters) from the time.

By carefully structuring a project so that students could think through into the past, the group can come to terms with the subject matter through drama. It goes almost without saying, of course, that children most readily identify and sympathise with historical characters of their own age.

Historical settings on the stage involve this amount of detail always. There is really no point in putting on a production of a play or musical set in the 19th century, typically *Oliver*, if the cast is dressed in varieties of ragged clothing with no design concept. Costume design should start in the present with an understanding of why people wear particular clothing and move backwards in time applying these principles to historic dress.

A performance project involved a group writing their own piece of music theatre about some 20th century children who travel back in time to a Victorian age. This was a useful exercise in that it combined the theatrical skills necessary to design for the present with settings in a Victorian period. Each character in the drama had characteristics: e.g. untidy, confident, rich, which were conveyed in the costume, but additionally some characters were Victorian. This gave opportunities for interaction between the characters of different times.

Scene 3: A Victorian street

Vicky and Liz are playing with a hoop. Enter Jackie.

JACKIE　**Oh, my head feels awful. (backs into Vicky) Sorry! Can you tell me where I am?**

VICKY　**Don't you know? We are in a street, of course (To Liz) Fancy not knowing that!...Silly person.**

JACKIE   **I only asked a civil question. The least you can do is give me a civil answer.**

LIZ   **All right, we will give you a civil answer. You-are-in-a-street.**

JACKIE   **Are you two going to a fancy dress party or something?**

LIZ   **Of course not! Everyone wears clothes like this, except beggars and scruffy boys like you.**

JACKIE   **I'm not a boy! I'm a girl.**

VICKY   **A girl? Dressed like that? You can't be. Why, you're wearing trousers and even they don't fit you. And that tunic is much too big for you. Can't you buy anything that fits you properly?**

LIZ   **He probably hasn't enough money.**

JACKIE   **I'm a girl, I tell you and for your information my clothes are meant to be baggy and my trousers are three quarter length. It's the latest fashion...**

Research was required to ensure that the music and settings were appropriate. This is the key to theatre design, understanding the need to design for characters first and not merely to design period costume.

Faces: a project about theatre make-up

1	Look at faces around us
My own face	Parts of a face/features
My friends' faces	What makes one face different from another?
Older people's faces	Teachers, parents. How can you tell age from a face?
Looking at a range of faces	Babies, infants, juniors, teenagers, adults. Drawings of example faces will be useful e.g. adult 'my Dad'
How do people alter their faces?	Make-up Camouflage Disguise (masks, glasses, hats, beards, moustaches)
What else can alter a face?	Weather (draw a girl in winter) Feelings (tears, smiles) Bruises, birthmarks, scars, cuts

2	Faces in the past
How can a face show a different period in time?	
Look at photographs of women from one family:	
	30 years ago
Now	What has changed?
60 years ago	Clothing? Make-up? Hairstyle? Style of photography? Expressions on faces?

3   Stage make-up

Stage make-up gives this an extra dimension. On stage you are trying to suggest many things about the personality of the character, set within an historical time. Thus the task is to design the face of a mother of five children, aged 42 years old, in 1917, living in the country in fairly poor conditions. You can see that to put such a character on stage involves a great deal of work! This is the sort of expertise needed for a professional make-up artist. In addition such a professional would need to have the technique to make up vast numbers of people in a small amount of time and in such a way that the make-up worked in the theatre.

This type of work helps children to think carefully about a particular time. So, work on make-up and wigs can help in an understanding of history.

It is essential to have a point of reference. The above discussions started from a photograph of a child of the same age and getting to know the child's family background and circumstances.

Environmental studies

A small primary school in Kent took on a project about insects. In line with good environmental studies practice, the teachers encouraged the children to look at insects and their habitat. This offered opportunities for all kinds of visual art, photography and other related work. The staff decided that each class would relate something of the outcome of their work to each of the other four classes in an end of term musical play. The staff allocated each class an area of insect life and each began to create a small theatrical scene for presentation. A narrative linked the scenes, this being a journey through the insect world by a child.

A professional set designer visited the school and talked to the children about his work in opera and ballet. Spontaneously he suggested to the groups that they might try to design their own ballet and opera and when asked about their topic work he found out about the insect project. As the term was nearing its end, the groups were all extremely well informed about their particular aspect of the insect world. So when they began to come up with ideas for the 'sets' their ideas were grounded in fact. They knew how to create the habitat for a dung beetle or butterfly. One 'world' included discarded coca-cola tins, litter and other rubbish. The exercise also enabled them to project the scale of such objects to the insect in question. When the sets were complete the classes were able to compare habitat with habitat and discuss their work intelligently. Also they were able to use the model sets to discuss how the scenes would be changed.

At this point set design became the servant of mathematics. A simple way to discuss scale is to suggest a scale (25 times bigger is most commonly used in theatres) and to ask simply; 'How big would you be if you were 25 times smaller? and your house? and a castle?' In the example of the insects, of course, the set design was scaling up! The grasses, weeds and dungheaps were made to look large against the small insects.

The Insect project was initiated as a science-based topic. Introduction of the arts element was by chance. However the set design work added:

- mathematical work in scaling up that would not have been incorporated otherwise.

- a fantasy element that allowed the children scope for imaginative writing within an area of growing expertise. Without the arts element the teachers might have been tempted to run a creative writing module alongside the insect project. As it was the children were able to write imaginatively about something that they had factual knowledge about. This is an important element of fiction.

The repertoire

We have mostly been concerned with creating new works and asking children about their own ideas. The theatrical repertoire does have a point of contact with the primary school, however. By the repertoire we tend to mean all operas, plays, ballets, musicals that are performed by professional companies. The repertoire would include everything from *Cats* and *Rigoletto* in the musical theatre to *Swan Lake* in ballet and *Abigail's party* or *Hamlet* in the straight theatre. Virtually anything, regardless of artistic merit, that is performed by professionals would be subsumed in this term. When a teacher books a set of tickets for her pupils to attend a performance she is, by virtue of government legislation, saying that the theatrical visit is part of the curriculum. How, then, can this be so?

It is unlikely that the average primary school will be studying set texts in the way that secondary schools, working on GCSE and 'A' level studies, would. However, going to see the 'set text play' is a very limited way of seeing the repertoire as an educational resource. What can a group of primary school children gain from going to see *The Firebird* by the Royal Ballet at Covent Garden? In this context the work needs to be treated as a springboard for cross-curricular classroom work.

The Firebird is the story of a magical bird who regains her freedom, from her captor, Prince Ivan, by giving him one of her feathers with which he will be able to call on her in any time of trouble. Subsequently the Prince falls in love with the Tsarevna, who has been captured by Kastchei, a monster. Kastchei is killed by Prince Ivan, with the assistance of the Firebird, and the prince and Tsarevna are able to marry. The ballet ends with an impressive procession.

This is a short ballet but, like another Stravinsky (operatic) score, *The Nightingale*, it is ideal for classroom treatment. The music is vivid and is broken up into identifiable scenes that the children can relate to and can easily identify when they see a performance. This type of work is useful *not* because it lends itself to an exposition of the piece from a musicological perspective but, rather, because it lends itself to the most creative type of cross-curricular work.

The Firebird herself is a good starting point. She has her own musical moments in the score and can be imagined by the children. They can start from Stravinsky's score, or better, project work could begin with merely the suggestion of the idea of a 'firebird' and the class could create their own music for the bird and some of the scenes in the ballet. Discussion about attitudes to 'fire' might be helpful and children could share any stories about fire that they know. It would be possible for groups to work on different composition and visual ideas with, perhaps, different instrumentation. Themes might be 'an enchanted garden', 'dance of the firebird', 'daybreak', 'Kastchei's monsters', 'procession'. Each piece of music should have a clear structure. In general when approaching any sort of writing it is helpful to divide the composition, however short, into a beginning, middle and end for, in dramatic terms, it is essential that there is a focal point for the action. The essence of drama is that there is a change in circumstances somewhere in the piece. In the case of *The Firebird* the situation at the beginning is, as it has been for some time, that the Tsarevna is controlled by Kastchei. The dramatic change occurs when Kastchei is killed. So in creating original music for the story there should be a distinction between scene setting music 'an enchanted garden', and music in which something of dramatic importance occurs.

Let's look at an example: *daybreak*

1   The composers' first job is to select appropriate instruments for themselves. It would be helpful to choose instruments that suggest daybreak in some way and also to select a variety of possible sounds.
2   Then it is necessary to create some moods in groups. From time to time the teacher might make suggestions or, better, ask helpful questions.
3   'Tunes' might be helpful and, if so, they can be 'banked' and when the piece is assembled they can be hinted at in the beginning section so that ideas can build.
4   Then a structure becomes necessary:
    Beginning: *end of the night*
    Middle: *daybreak* (dramatic moment)
    End: *day is established.*

Using the moods and the tunes a piece can be built up as an entirety.

Perhaps the tunes can be gradually assembled throughout the piece, ie. ideas only in Section 1, whole tunes in Section 2 and fragments again in Section 3. The mood music can also build and develop throughout the sections as necessary.

Once the music is written, or simultaneously, the dancing can be prepared. If the two are prepared at the same time the groups will be able to influence each other. In this way the dancing becomes fully integrated into the piece rather than dancing to accompany the music.

Take the firebird herself. How will she move? Will her costume affect her movements? If so, how? Will her movements be sharp or round? Will she be petite or statuesque? Build up a picture of her and prepare her movements in sections again. It is not necessary to have a narrative but a structure is helpful. The audience can then order its response. Recognition of earlier movements or particular responses to the music are comforting to the viewer. The firebird should have characteristics that are seen in her movements. She moves in a certain way because she is, for example, regal or powerful or good. In contrast Kastchei's movements should make the audience afraid and believe that the Tsarevna has no means of escape and that he has to be killed. It should be absolutely clear from the movements (aside from costuming) that these are very different types of characters.

To music and dance can be added drama to deal with the narrative sections (although in the ballet itself the whole story is danced). The opening scene in the forest and the procession might be pure drama. Consideration should be given to the setting. Could the firebird be represented by kathak dancing? There's no need at all for this sort of creative work to bear any relationship to the ballet itself. In fact it is better that there is a point for discussion in comparing the performance with the pupils' work and it is possible that the pupils will prefer their own 'treatment' of the story. Why not?

Try not to elevate Western art forms over others. If you're making suggestions about instrumentation or movement styles, try to be open. If you have access to recordings, videos, or professional assistance try to be diverse. Obviously any professional performance that the group sees will be an example of excellence in one form (e.g. ballet, Chinese theatre, mime) but the children should have access to as many as possible so that their minds are opened to the richness and diversity of the art forms of the world.

We have already discussed set design, make-up and costume in some detail so it is not necessary to recap, save to say that these fantastic creatures have *characteristics* and that they are probably more pronounced than in human characters. The firebird is an emblem of goodness and Kastchei evil. This should be brought out in the designs. Make-up designs would be great fun!

When the children see the stage production they will have gone through the thought processes that the composer, choreographer and designer went through. Consequently the children will be able to make sensible judgements about the success or otherwise of the piece and production. Rather than making bland comments about the piece, they will be perceptive about composer intention, design concept and choreography.

Sometimes teachers take the visit to a production a stage further and delve into historical background and other relevant details, for example making Russian food when going to see *Eugene Onegin*, recreating Viennese costumes for *Die Fledermaus* or project work on swans for *Swan lake*.

Theatre visits of this type, with the performance as a focus for classroom work, rely on a great deal of research and enthusiasm on the part of the teacher. They are, however, very refreshing to work on and many teachers enjoy the challenge of looking at a play, dance piece or opera with classroom work in mind. There are advantages of working in this way:

- there is a clear focus – going to a performance
- the children have an opportunity to work through some of the ideas in a piece and to share in the creative process as experienced by those associated with a production
- there is an opportunity to see the work of professionals and to look at it critically
- a project of this type provides a natural link across the subject areas.

Using professional artists and craftspeople in cross-curricular work

It is often useful to invite visitors to the school to help with cross-curricular work. Professional artists and craftspeople can either visit the school to talk about their work or, better, to perform or work alongside the children themselves. Visits to see the artists in their own environment are also very valuable and help to take the theatre work a stage further.

It can be difficult for a teacher to use professional skills of others within the classroom. Also professional artists are often only too aware that they don't have teaching skills (although animateurs often do). So how should the enthusiastic primary school teacher approach the professional world?

Almost all the major Arts Council funded arts institutions now run educational programmes. Such organisations include theatres, multi-arts centres, opera houses, ballet and dance companies and orchestras. Also for work with an historical perspective, many museums and galleries have excellent education programmes. The National Trust also encourages schools to use their properties as a resource.

Theatres

As well as the National Theatre and Royal Shakespeare Company, most of the regional theatres have educational programmes. Also regional theatres often have a policy on Theatre in Education (T.I.E.) and present programmes for pupils either in schools or in the theatre itself. Other bodies such as stately homes and the National Trust have T.I.E. terms.

In addition to actors working in schools there may be special performances at both local and national theatres that will be interesting to particular school groups. This could either be part of the company's repertoire (e.g. *The Pied Piper*) or a specially devised theatre piece that uses theatre as a means of instruction about another subject e.g. in science or on an environmental theme.

These can be valuable in emphasising the idea that theatre is about 'life' and is not only about things that happened in the past or fantasy.

Tours of theatres are fairly easily available. Most major London and regional theatres offer backstage tours and some commercial or small theatres will consider organising these if a request is made. Although some of the bigger theatres run tours throughout the working year and are accustomed to all levels of interest, the smaller theatres will often have to go to a great deal of trouble to offer a tour. In every instance the children will benefit from the visit if they are prepared for it. A group of infants visited the Royal Opera House model room having studied set design and costume. As the children knew something about set design they were able to ask interesting questions and, as a result, the team of professionals was able to discuss the work of a set designer in detail. Professionals in this sort of situation are not trained teachers and are often anxious about how to explain their work to a group of children.

- Most Arts Council funded theatres, performing companies and orchestras have a free mailing list for schools and send out information about performances at the theatres plus details of special projects in schools.
- In addition most companies often send out information packs to students on request or answer queries.
- Local theatres are keen to build up an audience for the future. Even if there isn't a special education programme, the theatre might be keen to develop links with local schools. Some theatre administrators will organise tours for class groups. Others might be willing for a small group to visit a particular department e.g. the public relations officer or the sound engineer.
- Teachers themselves can make contact with theatres on a personal level. At local level, theatre managements are often pleased to get some input from teachers about plays they would like to bring groups to, or to get an indication of general interest. Arts centres too are keen to hear from schools and colleges.
- It can also be useful for teachers and parents of a school to attend local theatre performances as part of the social side of the P.T.A.

6 Evaluation: the teacher's role

Often a teacher involved in a performing arts project will say that it would not matter if there were no performance as the children gain an enormous amount through the process of the project. This is fair comment and valid educationally. However, we must also consider how a project is perceived by the child. Children often fail to see an 'end' to any project. Often the time runs out: end of term, day, lesson, and a piece of work or project peters out too. There is no real sense of achievement for the group. Here is the strength of the performance as product. Although the educational process probably ends before the performance, the performance itself is the project's *raison d'être* for the group. So the two must be balanced carefully. If the process is too much in evidence there will no deadlines, no need for polish and rehearsal. If there is too much emphasis on the product the piece may be hurriedly put together without much educational outcome.

Let's look at the pros and cons:

Process

This is the educational reason for the project.

Too much emphasis on the process will:

- weaken the sense of deadlines and real achievement
- dilute the sense of the project for the students
- tend to leave the project unfocussed

Product

This is the point of the project for the students.

Too much emphasis on the product will:

- weaken the educational impact
- seriously affect the quality of the material presented
- lead to rushed work which takes little account of students' individual needs

The teacher can help the group to value the project work leading to a performance. For example, do visitors and school governors only attend final presentations and performances? Consider the following:

- try to invite governors and others associated with the school to see early project work as well as the final performance
- consider presenting a 'work in progress' to parents half way through the project
- share project work with other classes
- enable the children to see other class projects in progress
- encourage outsiders, other children and teachers to comment on 'work in progress' and encourage discussion within the classroom
- suggest that students introduce a performance with a short account of the full project.

One school term is an ideal time-scale for a performing arts project. The project can, if necessary, be broken up into modules which can each have its own beginning and end and obvious aims in terms of outcome. Modules can be by subject area or relating to a cross-curricular task.

Remember that there should be a balance between:

- creative work
- performance
- production
- critical work

It's not easy to ensure a balance of all four aspects for every child in every project, but a record of each child's work in each area is helpful. If, for example, a child has taken a major performance role in a project in the Autumn term it would be wise to involve him or her in a composition element in another project, perhaps a presentation in school assembly.

Over a school year the teacher can:

- create opportunities to present very short (1-5 minutes) pieces as well as longer ones
- suggest ways of developing ideas from other subject areas into presentations
- invite children to change roles within a project. If, for example, a group has been working on their own dance piece the teacher might suggest that the group could teach this to a second group.

Intensive arts weeks

Sometimes it is possible to create time for 'an intensive arts week'. This can be quite a good idea as it allows the children to focus on particular activities for longer stretches of time than would often be available. Also such a week can work exceptionally well if it coincides with the end of an on-going term long project. There are some dangers in this approach which are worth mentioning.

- If the 'intensive arts week' is the *only* arts activity in the school in a particular term, it can be perceived by the pupils as less serious than 'normal' work. Only when it enhances normal classroom work is it really useful. The sense of special occasion that is generated is important, but it is more valuable if the special arts week is an addition to normal work, not the only opportunity to be involved in the performing arts.
- Some teachers are tempted to take all the students out of their normal classroom environment and subject them to a flood of new activity. Some pupils find this disorientating. Also if students are allocated to particular areas within the arts, for example make-up, acting or set-design, bear in mind that while it is relatively simple to schedule a whole week on finding out about set design without any previous experience it might be less easy to find out 'all about make-up' for the same period.
- If the whole school is disrupted in this way it is essential to ensure that those teachers who are reluctant to get involved in the 'performing arts' but who, in order to make this type of week work, have to be included, feel secure and positive about the event.
- If the week is to result in a performance it has to be exceedingly well planned and co-ordinated. There is a problem if everyone is available for the whole week but the content of the performance is not known until mid-week and the costumes and props have to be ready for the dress rehearsal on the penultimate day, especially if those children doing set-design are not given a clear brief for the early part of the week. This results in time-wasting and boredom. An alternative is to stagger the 'week' over a longer period so that those aspects of the production that depend on ideas and/or script from another group start one or two days later.

The classroom space

The classroom is the environment in which the creative process and subsequent performances are nurtured. However, it is often difficult to ensure that a space is both a stimulating environment and a place for thinking, both a place to experiment and to perfect. Ideally there are spaces and equipment on hand in order to allow children to carry out their projects.

In the light of some of the ideas suggested earlier it's worth considering some questions.

- Is it possible for two or three composers to go off into a corridor or cupboard to try out a composition within earshot of the teacher?
- Is it possible for a group of 4 or 5 children to find a space to work on scenes through improvisation?
- If a child needs to listen to a tape of some previous work is there a tape-recorder at hand?
- Is it possible to make a word-processor or computer regularly available for writing and editing?
- Are there opportunities for children to work on acquiring skills independently of the project (e.g. to practise working out ideas in graphics in advance of preparing a poster)?
- Is there a model of the school's performing space in the classroom so that when any presentation, however small, is planned children can visualise how it will be set? (see below).
- Are musical instruments easily accessible? Is there a simple way of ensuring that these are replaced properly (e.g. a special cupboard where the absence of a xylophone is obvious)? Do all the pupils who are likely to use such instruments know how to put them away properly so that they are ready to use next time?
- Is there a supply of good quality materials for final versions of designs and publicity material, and a supply of suitable stationery for rough versions?

Equipment

Very little special equipment is needed for a performing arts project. Any space, however simple, can become a performing space. However, if the school wants to invest in some special equipment there are some useful items available. Buying equipment for performing arts work in the school should be linked to a 'whole school policy'. It's sad to see primary schools equipped with expensive drama equipment which is no longer used because the member of staff who ordered it has moved on.

Basic equipment might include some of the following:

stra or stage blocks are very useful as these allow the designers to work with different levels. Make sure that the ones you buy are easily portable by groups of children and aren't too difficult to get out and pack away. Most can be bought a few at a time and some come in an assortment of shapes and sizes so that you can have steps and slopes.

If you invest in rostra make a point of making up a set of miniature rostra (to scale) and a model child (again in scale) and let the children experiment with the shapes in a classroom model box. They will soon learn what effects can be achieved with the blocks, without heavy lifting work. Also make a virtue out of necessity. Some very lively performances have used wall bars as part of a set, or a canteen hatch in the design.

Simple stage lighting adds more to a production than any other item of equipment. Start with lighting instruments that can blanket light the stage area rather than spotlights. Ideally you need a lighting board of some sort so that the lights can be cued. A lighting board allows the lights to be organised from one place. A pupil can have a script and can operate the lights by following the lines with lighting cues written in. Some lighting made for school use has a dimmer switch attached to individual lights so that a pupil can stand by each one with the controls and turn lights on, off or up or down. A dimmer board works on exactly the same principle as a household dimmer switch. Coloured gels add atmostphere. Get a selection of colours and let the children experiment. How can a colour change the mood? Red is often used to suggest evil, for example.

Black-out curtains are essential if you're using lighting, as many school performances take place during daylight hours. Ideally curtains should be lined and not too patterned. Most school curtains, if lined, are effective as a blackout. Any curtaining that doesn't allow light through will be suitable as long as it suits school safety standards. Schools with roof windows create a real problem and it might be worth painting them black if the hall is regularly used for performances. Black venetian blinds are good when new but seem to have a short life. Curtaining and blinds can be bought from the better school suppliers.

A good selection of musical instruments is necessary and can include untuned percussion (tambourines, wood blocks) tuned percussion (xylophones, glockenspiels) and other instruments (keyboards, recorders). Good quality instruments are more satisfying to play, so if money is short devise a policy of buying a small number of instruments each year. This ensures that there is a steady flow of new instruments that the children haven't used before. Also bear in mind that some music advisers have a supply of instruments that can be borrowed for specific projects and can augment the existing supply. Experiment with unusual instruments and those from non-European traditions.

A word processor or computer is a very useful item. It enables scripts to be written and edited easily. Often schools use word processors to produce press releases, scripts and programmes. Software is available for composition purposes and for notating and producing parts. Graphic images can also be produced. Anita Straker discusses the use of computers and the creative arts in *Children using computers* (Blackwell, 1989).

A good quality sound system enables the use of cassettes during a performance. Children can record music or sound effects to be played during a piece. Any dance work performed to taped music is enhanced by good quality sound reproduction. The tape operator should stand by the recorder during the performance and use the script for cues.

Methods of recording performances and work in progress such as **cameras** and **video cameras** are useful to have, especially if the children themselves are encouraged to use them. Video helps to encourage self-criticism and performer effectiveness.

Cassette tape-recorders and personal stereos are useful, particularly if they are used throughout the school and the children get used to them being available. These can be used to record work or to play commercially-produced tapes. Also children can record composition work and send it to another group or class to use for dance or drama.

Responsibility and safety

When children are encouraged to act on their own initiative and to take responsibility for carrying out a task, they need to know of any essential safety rules.

Here are some simple rules:

- Access to equipment and materials needs to be easy but children must take responsibility for putting things away properly.
- The work area should be left clean and tidy at the end of each session.
- Careful rules regarding electricity should be followed, especially where stage lighting is involved. Children should not plug in

stage lighting without supervision and should turn lights on and off at the switch, not the plug. Some local authorities will not allow children to operate stage lighting at all.

• Cables needed for lighting instruments should be taped to the floor and labelled.

• Any other school safety rules should be followed carefully.

Materials

Materials including junk of all sorts, as well as high quality art materials are essential. A major difference between amateurs and professionals is the quality of materials they use. So it is preferable to have one good quality set of materials to be shared rather than a class set of poor items. Infants, for example, produce excellent art work with inks or pastels, yet often powder paint or its equivalent seems to be the only paint available to them. From an early age children can have access to, and learn to respect, high quality tools, materials and instruments. This links with the workshop atmostphere of the classroom. One reason for using cheap materials is in order to keep up with the enormous output of work. Children in primary school can 'turn out' dozens of paintings and examples of written work. The workshop atmosphere enables the student to differentiate between the technique learning and developing process and the end product. Each task, for example, in design or music composition, can be worked at, refined, discussed, adjusted, improved in its early stages. Hence, in design, the importance of the white card model. This is not just an arbitrary stage but enables the pupil to work through the problem before embarking upon the next important stage of the completed model.

Assessment

The subject of assessment and evaluation in arts education is a continuing area of debate. On the one hand people say that there is no effective way of evaluating the arts, while on the other it is suggested that there could be a universal system of graded tests for arts subjects, in a similar way to those that are commonly set in practical music teaching. In other words, at one extreme of the argument there is pure instinct and at the other a technique that can be evaluated in exactly the same way as any other examinable subject. As usual there is something to be said for both positions but let's examine the arguments more carefully.

The arts can, of course, be about natural talent. No one could helpfully deny that there are some people with natural ability in the arts. If, however, any evaluation is carried out with this as a primary consideration then there can be little point in *teaching* the arts in schools at all. If one is to teach successfully, it is essential that there is some measure of progress on the part of those involved in the learning experience. Further it is important that the arts experiences that occur throughour a child's school career are not just assumed to be 'a good thing' because 'it was obvious' or 'they talked about it for weeks afterwards'. Many quite dubious experiences would have the same effect!

Evaluation is also important in terms of the status of arts work. Traditionally in secondary schools, it is subjects like maths, science and English that have been better serviced and funded because they have been seen as core areas of the curriculum. The arts on the other hand have been seen by some as the province only of the primary school and those involved in the 'school play'. If, in primary schools, there is a belief that the arts subjects are in some way unable to be assessed, or pupils' work evaluated, there is an assumption that the teaching of such subjects is of lesser value than for a subject where there is testing.

Those connected with the school can be involved in the debate about the importance of the arts. School governors, parents and friends of the school need to be aware of the policy on arts education in the school. Any literature about the school needs to include this area of work.

When we talk of evaluation there are three areas to consider:

1 Is the pupil benefitting from the performing arts programme both generally (bearing in mind what has been said about integrating other work into an arts programme), and in relationship to particular objectives in the individual arts subject areas in line with the aims set out by the school as a whole?

General benefits might include:

problem solving abilities
sensitivity to subject material
responses to work of others

Subject specific attainments could be:

technical ability within dance, music or drama
facility to create new material within the form

2   Is the arts programme itself effective? Has a useful way of working been achieved? Is it possible to improve the content of arts work in the school?

3   In the long term is the 'whole school policy' working well for all the students?

4   Are members of staff working together?

Objective and subjective

An awareness of objective and subjective assessment and evaluation is important. Often these seem to be presented as *either* subjective *or* objective. Some people strive for an objective model of evaluation that seeks to describe a project or pupil and then to measure it against a set of objective criteria. Others claim that this is impossible and that only subjective measures are possible. There is a place for both. In general, objective testing or assessment will *tend* to be of most use where comparisons are made, and subjective evaluation will tend to question the nature of the activity.

Care should be taken about any objective evaluation of the child's material or output, as this should always be put in a context. Too often the emphasis is put on the end product and it is quite possible for individuals to turn out excellent work in the arts without any evidence of progress at all. The child who can play an instrument, sing well or dance will be able to produce attractive or skilful work with very little effort and to order. This is why it is essential to look at the context. *The key to evaluation is the possibility of change.* Evaluation takes place in order both to ask pertinent questions about the environment in which the learning is taking place, and to explore ways of becoming more effective. In the unlikely event of a teacher having a set programme that has 'worked' for years and having no intention of changing it, any exercise in evaluation would be useless. Evaluation is an on-going process involving an examination of what is going on and an intelligent questioning of why.

Also any evaluation process is itself in a context. What is a 'good' result in 1989 will not be appropriate in 1999 and would not have been appropriate in 1979. Evaluation takes on new thinking, trends in the art-forms, the interests of young people, the needs of the group, class or school as a whole.

In the student the process should be diagnostic. There is no obvious body of knowledge as such to be tested but rather the child should be observed to see how she is thinking, working or acting and, in terms of what one has learned to expect of the child or group, whether she is continuing to make progress.

So there are two aims:

* to assess progress on the part of the child.
* to assess effectiveness in terms of the teaching situation and the task itself

There is little point at looking at the product itself in objective terms although, as discussed in an earlier chapter, this will be of major importance to the child.

There are three groups of people involved in the evaluation process:

* the students themselves for whom methods of self-assessment (such as pupil booklets described below) are useful
* the teacher who is trying to match the pupils' abilities with the tasks set but who is also involving him or herself in self-assessment in terms of the teaching process
* the parents who will be interested in their own child's progress and can, if included in this process, add to the success of the work
* Also in a subsidiary role any outside professional artists involved in projects can, in a discreet way, encourage the evaluation process

In chapter 1 we said that an arts project should have four aspects:

* creative
* re-creative
* skills and technique
* critical ability.

Each of these four areas should be evaluated and further there should be an acknowledgement of the type of learning going on, i.e. the arts should evoke a response *intellectually, emotionally* and *physically*. Dance, for example, should not be about 'pure technique', encouraging only the learning of steps but should also be about what is being communicated and motivation.

Student diaries or record books

It should be possible for the pupils themselves to be party to an evaluation and to record their own thoughts about the project, ideas about their own achievement and considered opinion about the project as a whole. A fairly common and very useful way of conducting this sort of self-evaluation is for the pupils themselves to keep working diaries during the progress of a project. These should be kept carefully but should not reduce the whole experience to 'writing about' what has happened. It has been said that often performing arts work appeals to those children who are not *necessarily* good in reading and writing-related subject areas, and to reduce a project that such a child is succeeding in, to yet more writing could destroy its value to that child. There are other ways of recording feelings and ideas. Individual diaries might, for example, include large numbers of photographs. A camera is a very useful classroom tool and albums of photos (if funds allow) can work in a similar way to holiday photograph albums. The child can caption the pictures and describe them to interested adults. This enables the child to think back over the project and to see from where she started and contrast this with the point she has reached towards the end of the project.

Working charts, lists and other materials can be preserved. Handwriting and presentation are not so important here but the fact that the particular page is destined for such a record book will ensure more care is taken with such materials. Costume lists, cast lists, copies of a press-releases, working scripts, melodies – all such items can be kept. Record books of this type should be carefully bound so that they have a clear status. If the school has a policy on such individual record-keeping, students will accept it as a normal part of school life. Such documents are very useful when sharing a child's work with parents as they can see the range of cross-curricular work involved in an arts project and can monitor progress. If children are allowed to take such diaries home, either on a daily basis or at certain agreed times (perhaps monthly or at the end of each term) they can provide a subject for family discussion. Teachers can request parent comment if this can be organised within the spirit of the record-keeping i.e. to further the project. This work should be kept up throughout the project so that it encourages a constant self-assessment in the child and a feeling of achievement.

Teachers who read the entries to diaries will be able to see a project or scheme from the child's viewpoint. This is helpful when devising new work and can suggest ways of presenting material, explaining the point of a particular piece or programme of work. Also much of what pupils record will take the form of recording rather than evaluation. This material can be used by the teacher for purposes of evaluation.

Exhibitions

Some teachers prefer to keep such material for a large exhibition rather than individual record books. This has the disadvantages of not 'belonging' to the individual children but the advantage of bringing all the work together so that the scope of what has been undertaken and that material common to a group of children (e.g. the set design) can be presented jointly. The sheer amount of such a body of work is always impressive to the students but, naturally, a large amount of teacher time goes into mounting such an exhibition! Children can, of course, help with the presentation of their own work. Work should be respected in the way in which it is mounted. Ideas can be found by looking at major retrospective exhibitions mounted by galleries and museums. Certain items are given extra status by their positioning and mounting. In this case the set design, photographs of rehearsals, important events, costume drawings might have attention drawn to them, whereas the background work might be mounted in a different way. The hidden statement would be that much work has been done for the particular performing arts project but that much of the work has not appeared on stage and has, in fact, been discarded in favour of other ideas. As in a gallery exhibition, sources and early sketches would be differentiated from studies and completed pieces.

Again through a 'whole school policy' on this type of presentation, the children will soon learn to put their own work in context, not in a competitive way (by comparing their own work unfavourably) but in a positive way (seeing other people's ideas). They will also know that it is school practice to make sure that early work is preserved for display later. If exhibitions following creative arts projects are regularly mounted in schools it would be useful to organise occasional visits to major retrospective exhibitions in galleries, ('Hockney paints the stage' would be an obvious example of a past exhibition). This would enable children to see how a professional artist's work is presented (including cards and catalogues) and how such an exhibition is reviewed in the national press.

Making connections with the constant assessment of professional work in this way (including newspaper, radio and T.V. reviews of performances) gives value to the assessment process and creates discussion. If, for example, a class visit to a new production of a ballet was organised, the teacher could collect newspaper reviews for classroom use after the visit and could share any radio review. Archivists in theatres can sometimes supply photocopies of reviews of past productions, and historical evidence about the première of the work is usually widely available on the reception. Such documentary evidence can be displayed alongside any work by the children. Again this develops the project further. The work by the students stands alongside popular assessments in the past and present and the pupils will see further productions in this context.

It is helpful if a folder or special cupboard is made available for the storage of early drafts, photographs, sketches and other material so that these items can be gathered together at the end of a term or project. Exhibitions of work *encourage* the children and give them a sense of pride in their work.

Sharing of work

Sometimes the results of a project mounted by several classes will be brought together in a 'sharing event'. Such a 'showing of work' is an excellent end to a performing arts project. A session might involve each class explaining how a piece came about and then a short performance. Ideally there will be opportunities to consider the pieces in discussion, or for a teacher to comment positively. Such sessions leave the children with more to think about. A session could conclude with a short demonstration by older children and/or professionals. A 'sandwich' presentation by students and professionals is always exciting but, of course, relies on the availability of outsiders. Even when there is no comment within the presentation itself, it is useful for individual classes to discuss other children's work as this is a vital aspect of developing 'critical' skills. Again a 'whole school policy' helps here. Over a number of years in a school, children will learn that there is room for positive discussion about work done. They will not feel vulnerable or protective about particular ideas nor will they make spiteful comments. They will learn that material can be subject to debate and analysis.

A pattern of questioning helps. Compare:

What did you think of Class 5's presentation?

with

How do you think Class 5 composed their piece?

and

Did you like . . . ?

with

Why did the first section seem frightening?

There should be opportunities for children to discuss a performing arts project with their teachers and others involved, after a performance. Ideally this should be a day or so after the final presentation. Children can be reminded of the stages of the project and asked for their feelings about each one.

- remind the children of the starting points for the project

We started this project with a blank sheet of paper. I didn't think we would ever do it.

- remember any special visits or visitors associated with it

It was exciting when the dancers came to our school. The man was so strong. He lifted the lady right over his head.

- ask them about their own part in the project

I wrote to all the newspapers in the Yellow pages. I wrote to Prince Charles and Princess Diana. When the letter came back Mrs. Potter put it on the wall.

- invite them to comment on any other pupils who have helped them in the project

Kerry wrote a lot of the songs. I helped her with one and I wrote one on my own. Kerry liked my song.

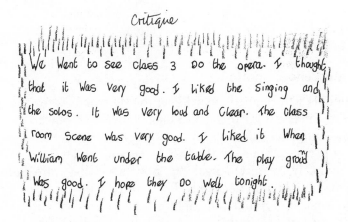

Critique

We Went to see class 3 Do the opera. I thought that it Was Very good. I liked the singing and the solos. It Was Very loud and Clear. The class room Scene Was Very good. I liked it When William Went under the table. The play groud Was good. I hope they Do Well tonight.

Figure 23 *Not only are other children's comments interesting to read, they also create a sense of comradeship. Everyone wants the play to go well.*

- accept any feedback from the students

Everyone was excited as the play got on the way. At the beginning I thought it was hanging too much on the teachers. We seemed to be getting nowhere as if we were walking through thick mud.

I thought learning the words would be much harder but we practised before just making up the words to go with the story so when we came to learn the words it was easy.

Now I understand what composers do. They make up music in their minds.

The first stages [of the project] were slow. Until one day we were told we only had a few weeks left. Now we had to get our skates on. We practised hard the next few weeks.

I think we did very well and if we had the time I would like to do it again.

It was the best thing I have ever done

The teacher and school

A 'whole school' policy

Most schools will require record-keeping by teachers for this type of project and it is useful to have a clear outline of objectives (school and class side by side so that an individual teacher's objectives mirror the wider aims of the whole school policy) and a regular (daily, monthly, termly) check on how well these are being met. Objectives should not be fixed. They should be capable of adjustment so that individual abilities can be stretched and advantage taken of any arts activity in the local area, visits by performers to the school or theatre trips. Graded tests bring with them the danger of 'teaching down' i.e. determining what a particular age-group should *know* or be able to do (e.g. be able 'to demonstrate an interest in...') and not taking a particularly able child on from that point. Also there's the danger of privileging skills outlined in plans of objectives above other skills or ideas that might be topical or hold the interest of the pupils more clearly.

The skilful teacher will be able to put objectives into perspective. By evolving a diagnostic approach to work in class he or she will be able to have the aims of the 'whole school policy' very clearly in mind the entire time but will be able to realise its aims in a number of different ways. Also it should be possible to think about the

1

The Opera in Retrospect

Looking back on the opera now, I didn't realise how much hard work, determination, spare time, people thinking for themselves and people sparing things for our benefit it would mean. My job was production manager which was the person who was overall in charge of the company, apart from Mr. Fell and Mrs. Curtis, the two teachers for class 5 and 6, who were the two directors for our company.

We started off by choosing the jobs we would like to do. There were eleven categories, make-up designers, costume designers, technicians, composers, writers, set designers, public relations, stage managers, production manager, and directors but that job had already been taken and the last job, acting.

Many people had to do two jobs or even three. In my booklet, which I was given by the directors, it said that I was to work with the actors as little as possible. I worked quite a lot with the set designers near the performance time because they were very behind on their work schedule for painting the scenery and I also worked quite a bit

2

with the the public relations team by helping design the posters, dictate letters to the press and other people, helping with the Box Office team inviting people in to the performances, helping keep count of the money and when the performances were over, deciding what bills we had to pay off, such as the use of the photocopyer, all the paper we used and bunches of flowers for Mrs. Carty, Mrs. Brett and Mrs. Leng.

In my job I had to make quite a lot of decisions but I got help from the directors, sometimes. I had a great deal of responsibility too, like if the designs for make-up weren't jazzy enough for the freedom fighters and it was too bright for the Victorians. The costume designers, I had to tell them that the future costumes were too plain and dull, and so on. Many other people probably thought that their jobs were the hardest, and I thought my job was the hardest but if everyone hadn't done their job properly the opera would not have become what it is now

Gary
Collins.

Figure 24 *Reviewing the whole project reminds everyone of what has been achieved and can inform the teachers about how the pupils saw it.*

curriculum *as a whole*. Thus, for music, an aim might be to introduce children to a selection of different composers' work but this could be achieved through story telling. There could be opportunities for children to go to a tape-recorder with headphones (or as a class group) to listen to such works as *Peter and the wolf* or *The Firebird* as programme music and not as an aspect of a performing arts programme. Similarly a mathematical objective might be to understand the use of scale but this could be achieved through the preparation of a model box for a school play. The teacher has to be in command of the various activities going on but shouldn't be blinkered in thinking about aims within subject barriers but rather within the wider context of the curriculum itself.

A diagnostic approach

If there is an atmosphere in which the teacher is looking for weaknesses and filling in with skills teaching, there will be opportunities to organise short projects which will assist and enhance other work. Practical 'problems' which act as skills sessions will be useful.

A *design* problem might be to consider how to create a sense of space and of claustophobia on stage. To experiment in this way it's essential to have a model box. Make a set of three-dimensional shapes over a period of time that can be used in the model box to create such environments, so that when exercises of this type are useful there is always a box and some shapes available. The shapes mentioned can be used to denote space or claustrophobia, power or equality.

Other design exercises might use the shapes to create:

* chaos
* order
* freedom
* disorder

This method of taking groups off for specific exercises that will later enhance the main project makes use of a workshop environment in the classroom. Materials need to be readily available so that a diagnostic approach to learning can be used by the teacher. For example if a weakness in understanding design becomes apparent when a small group is working, they should be able to go off to a corner where there is a series of 3-D shapes to experiment with. Similarly there should be corridors or large cupboards where a group can try out musical ideas without disturbing the rest of the class. In

Thankyou for teaching
us how to play so well
together it was a wounderful
feeling when everything went
so smoothly I certainly
learnt a lot of new ways
of expressing myself in the
music thankyou

Melanie Crawford
— x —

(musician)

I have enjoyed doing
the play with you, it
has been a great laugh
and that Saterday was
really good when we made
sid.
thank you very mutch
for picking us for the project.
yours sincerely
Dean Hollis
carpenter

Figure 25 *A good project leaves children feeling 'special'.*

many primary schools it is common to see children busy composing in corridors all over the school.

From time to time it is worth reviewing National Curriculum guidelines against the individual pupil's skills. Imagine some typical attainment targets:

• Do the pupils understand how to produce a chronological narrative?

Script writing is perfect for this. It allows children to think in sections: beginning, middle and end, in three scenes which can be in three different settings with a developed narrative. Having produced a piece for performing, a written story will be easier.

• Do pupils understand scale?

They can produce a scale drawing of the performing area which can be incorporated into a model box.

• Can the pupil use a word processor for editing purposes?

Suggest that a student prepare a programme for a performance. A first draft can be prepared and discussed with the actors, and amendments made before a final version of it is printed to distribute to the audience.

Staff development

The teacher will progress too! If the teacher himself is gaining an interest in the wider arts world and is becoming more competent within the field of organising arts projects this will be an invaluable asset! The availability of books, videos, teaching materials and courses helps here, as does the interaction with the major and local theatre companies.

Evaluation can lead to the teachers in a school recognising the need for outside help in a particular area of work. Perhaps it might be helpful for the whole staff to visit a local theatre to see backstage, or even to attend a theatre performance as a group. If a group of children have booked to see a performance it might be possible for a group of teachers to go to an earlier performance or rehearsal and then discuss the piece. This would enable another teacher (other than the class teacher) to discuss the visit with the pupils later. Schools wishing to organise their productions along the lines of a professional theatre might invite a stage manager to visit the school to speak to the staff. Teachers often invite interesting people to their schools to talk to pupils but not so often to meet the staff. Such

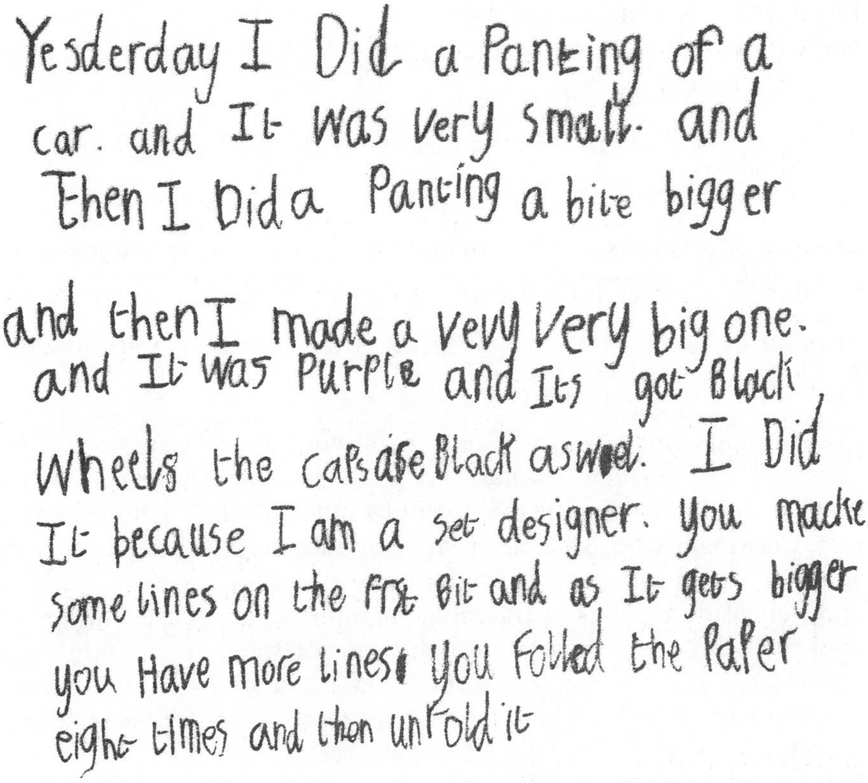

Yesderday I Did a Panting of a
car. and It was very small. and
Then I Did a Panting a bite bigger

and then I made a vevy very big one.
and It was Purple and Its got Black
wheels the caPs are Black as wel. I Did
It because I am a set designer. you made
some lines on the Frst Bit and as It gets bigger
you Have more lines you Folled the PaPer
eight times and then unfold it

Figure 26   *What seems like an exciting painting project achieves understanding of size and scale in mathematics.*

a visit puts the outside professional, who is probably not accustomed
to meeting children, at ease, as well as informing both interested
and as yet uninterested teachers.

In-service days provide an excellent opportunity for the whole staff
to invite professional artists to visit their school for a day and to
work alongside them in devising a performing arts programme.
Alternatively they can ask professionals to visit the school to tell
them about opportunities available, or even to explain in more
detail some of the ideas mentioned above.

Programmes for such days might look something like this:

Example 1 An introduction to opera for primary schools

Session 1: What is theatre design? (practical workshop by theatre set and/or costume designer)

Session 2: Interpretation: singing a role in opera (demonstration by an opera répétiteur and singer)

Session 3: A director's role (practical workshop by stage director)

Example 2 Creating music-theatre in the classroom

Session 1: Introduction to composition (professional composer)

Session 2: Subject for writing (session with director or writer)

Session 3: Composing and rehearsal (with composer and director)

Session 4: Showing of work

Professionals work best with teachers when there is a clear aim. They are not teacher trainers and, at best, can share their own specific skills with teachers who will be able to adapt them for their own classroom use. Also there are animateurs who present work-shops for performing arts companies and other arts organisations and Education Officers in theatre companies who would be happy to advise on this type of event. It is helpful for the staff to build up a list of local and national contacts (artists and advisers) who might be willing to visit the school either once or on a regular basis. Many people are happy to do this free of charge.

Student response to arts projects

There will be times when the pupils take the project on beyond the teacher's expectations. If, for example, a project has been organised along the lines of a professional performing company, then it is often the case that a child taking on a particular role will exceed the brief with dramatic effect. The press officer or stage manager might act in a truly professional way. Perhaps the marketing officer might suggest that to create company unity, t-shirts might be produced! The teacher should challenge the idea, outline problems and send the 'Marketing Manager' away to work out the difficulties and present a case! Initiative in fulfilling an arts task should be encouraged at all levels.

The teachers together need to see the overview and need to share notes regularly so that over a period of years in the school, the pupils will take on different roles. Each project will have creative and practical aspects but each child does not necessarily have to work in both areas in every project. If, however, a child has worked on costume design over an extended period there should be opportunities in another project for him or her to work in a different area. Ideally pupils who do take on the role of costume designer in a later project will share the experience with that child. Also a 'whole school policy' should take account of particular skills and interests of the staff. If a particular teacher has an interest in dance and another in music there might be an emphasis on these areas in certain years or opportunities to bring the appropriate classes together for team teaching at particular times.

Short, medium and long term evaluation

- In the *short term* the teacher should be able to assess immediate responses in the students on a day to day basis.
- In the *medium term* it should be possible to detect advance.
- In the *long term* there should be some clear indications that the student has carried out and profited by a *balanced* arts programme.

Profiling for the teacher is very much based on similar ideas to the student diaries mentioned above. It allows the teachers in a school to document what progress has been made in the area of arts education. The individual record on any one student, however, must be placed in the context of evaluation of the project itself. Did the task stretch the pupil? Was there a real sense of achievement at the end? Was it clear that something tangible in terms of skills learning took place? Was there a balance between a project that stretched the pupils' abilities and the need to enable them to feel secure in the learning experience?

The important point is balance. It is the teacher's responsibility to ensure in the short term (day to day and termly) that his or her pupils are getting a balanced arts programme that is demanding and stretching. The school policy also has to be examined to ensure that performing arts are given enough attention.

Creative aspects of a project

- Pupils can be monitored to ensure that they build on what has been done before and that later tasks, for example attempts with the same medium, build on that progress. The teacher can ensure that students are able to work creatively in several forms; dance, drama, music, art, multi-media.
- Individual pupils should be encouraged to develop creative ideas

and not to skip from project to project. A student who, with a group, has worked on a music composition project might be given the task of writing another piece of music specifically to be choreographed or to accompany a piece of mime. In this way the student can begin where he or she left the last project rather than starting all over again.

- Occasionally a task might be set to show the pupil how far he or she has developed within a certain timescale. It's not always necessary to start again with new material.

Much of what has been discussed seems time consuming. It's essential to devise as many ways as possible of making both recording and evaluation as painless and trouble-free as possible. This is why a whole school system is essential. Teachers can devise their own methods of assessment, recording and evaluation that will build into a whole school system. Avoid lengthy photocopied sheets that have large sections to be filled in.

Consider:

- Is it possible to record information 'on the spot', when the children are present?
- Does the teacher prefer to sit down quietly with papers in the evening?

Both will have a place but there is a clear need to find a way of both describing and evaluating work that fits in with the teacher's preferred methods of work. Teachers use a variety of recording methods. Suggestions have been:

- keeping a page-a-day diary on a teacher's desk so that impressions, needs and achievements can be jotted in note form (Sam asked about videoing his work/Sita said her uncle would visit the school to talk about his poetry/Jason had difficulty reading the instruction card). Such notes can be referred to at the end of the term or year.
- lesson notes, aims and objectives held on a word-processor can be copied and edited for preserving at the end of the school year. Comments can be incorporated in a different typeface showing what has been achieved. A school diary, for example, might be worth keeping.

Evaluation is about common sense. Like critical skills it often, at best, looks after itself. If the teacher and school have clearly defined aims, organise their time and classrooms to assist the learning experience and set up projects with real tasks and deadlines they will often evaluate their work automatically. For those that need to think more formally, the key is to think of evaluation as diagnostic: to continually question everything done in the classroom and to consider other ways of achieving the objectives. At heart it is essential to ensure that each pupil is working within a clearly defined structure in a way that stretches his or her individual abilities.

```
                              CHIPSTIX

                  Financial Statement for the Production of

                              TIME KIDS
                  ==========================================


INCOME                                   EXPENDITURE
======                                   ===========
                                       !                              !
Ticket Sales :-              £0.00 !                          £0.00 !
             Adult   Child         !Makeup           16.63        !
Tues          45      29     29.75 !                 14.15       30.78 !
Wed           47      28     30.50 !                              !
Thurs         60      28     37.00 !Flowers                      15.30 !
             ------------------    !                              !
             152      85           !Costumes          7.93        !
                                   !                  1.05        8.98 !
Door Sales    14       5      8.25 !                              !
             ------------------    !Music                         0.58 !
      total  166      90           !                              !
                                   !Paper & Stationery 5.00       !
Price        0.50    0.25          !                   5.20      10.20 !
                                   !                              !
                                   !Stamps                        5.40 !
Other Receipts                5.40 !                              !
                                   !Profit                       39.66 !
                            =========!                       =========!
                            110.90 !                         110.90 !
                            =========!                       =========!


Transactions to be completed :-

    1) Pay £2-00 into bank
    2) Pay £10-20 to School


                  Statement of account prepared by Jonathan P. Foster

                  Head of Public Relations


                      Jonathan Foster
                  ........................
                  11 May 1987
```

Figure 27 *Could this degree of mathematical understanding have been achieved through exercises?*

Finally it is necessary to define *achievable aims* and to take stock of what has been achieved at the end of each week, term and year. These need to be considered alongside the proposals for the National Curriculum and should take some of the following into account:

- the aims of the school arts policy
- the project work planned by individual teachers and its effectiveness
- the response to planned work by both individual students and groups
- the response of individuals and groups over a longer period of time
- the ability and achievement of pupils
- attainment targets identified by the teacher, the school, the Local Authority advisers and HMI

Notes

For a detailed project analysis see *Classroom issues in assessment and evaluation in the arts* Berkshire LEA SCDC Arts in Schools Project 1989.

Glossary of technical terms to introduce to children

Teachers requiring more detailed information at their own level should refer to the various dictionaries of theatre, ballet and opera available: Oxford University Press has published such dictionaries for opera and ballet and a companion to the theatre.

Auditions: a way of choosing the performers: usually the director will audition actors and if singing or dancing is required the musical director/conductor and/or choreographer will also be involved

Auditorium: the part of the theatre where the audience sits

Ballet: a piece of theatre involving 'classical' choreography

Blocking: the 'moves' given to an actor by a director

Call-sheet: a schedule of rehearsals given by the stage-manager to the company

Choreography: the process of creating a dance or ballet

Choreographer: the person who creates a dance or ballet

Company Manager: the person who looks after the actors, singers and staff. The Company Manager sometimes takes charge of the PR

Composer: the person who creates a piece of music

Conductor: the person in charge of the orchestra (usually also the Musical Director)

Costume: what the actors wear

Costume Designer: The person who designs the costumes for a play, opera or ballet. This will usually include wigs (if any), hairstyle, make-up, shoes, jewellery etc.

Critic: a professional critic views a production at a press evening (often the first public performance) and writes a review for newspaper or journal

Dimmer: an electrical gadget which enables the lights to be 'dimmed'

Director: the person who, through his or her work with the actors and other members of the company, interprets the play for the audience

Duet: musical section for two singers (also trio for three, quartet for four etc. A piece for several singers is called an ensemble)

Front of House: the area of the theatre used by the audience

Front of House staff: people with responsibility for looking after the audience: House Manager, Press Officer, Box Office staff, Marketing department etc.

Libretto (pl. libretti): the script (see below) of an opera

Musical: a piece of theatre with musical moments where the action is interrupted for a 'number'

Notation: the means of recording music or dance

Opera: a piece of theatre involving music and theatre. The chief distinction between opera and musicals is where they are performed .and how perceived by the public at large. In general operas would tend to present a more integrated music theatre piece than a musical

Orchestra: a group of players providing the music for a performance

Overture: an introductory piece of music which sometimes includes musical ideas that will be heard later in the piece

Plot: what happens in a play

Production: a production is an interpretation of a piece of theatre or dance with a 'new' concept from the director: this would usually involve completely new sets and costumes. Subsequent performances of the same production but rehearsed at another time would be termed a 'revival'

Production Manager: The person in charge of the production who makes sure everything is built, organised and paid for

Props: short for properties and including anything used on stage other than scenery, furniture or costumes

Repertoire: Plays that are performed by a particular company are said to be in that company's repertoire

Repertory system: the system whereby a number of works are said to be in a company's repertoire and are performed on and off throughout a given season

Revival: See Production, any subsequent production of a new work is, technically, a revival

Rostrum: a stage block providing a raised area

Script: the words of a play

Score: the musical 'script'

Set Designer: The person who arrives at a visual concept (or idea) for a play, opera or ballet. The Set Designer is usually responsible for the set or scenery and sometimes acts as Costume Designer also

Sitzprobe: a singing rehearsal; usually an opportunity for a complete sing-through without acting or moving

Stage Manager: the person who is in charge of the stage and runs the performances. The Stage Manager attends all rehearsals and marks any 'moves' and 'blocking' in his or her script. If the director is not available, the stage manager can run rehearsals. If there is a Deputy Stage Manager he or she will probably 'prompt' and take charge of props. There can be also be Assistant Stage Managers

Wardrobe Director: the person in charge of the 'running wardrobe' (looking after the completed costumes during the performances not the making of the costumes for the production which is done by the Costume Designer and/or 'production wardrobe')

Index